SUBNORMAL

How I Was Failed By The British Education System And A Colonial Family: The Windrush Generation

MAISIE BARRETT

Copyright © 2023
MAISIE BARRETT
SUBNORMAL
How I Was Failed By The British Education System And A Colonial Family: The Windrush Generation
All rights reserved.

No part of this publication may be reproduced, distributed, or transmitted in any form or by any means, including photocopying, recording, or other electronic or mechanical methods, without the prior written permission of the publisher, except in the case of brief quotations embodied in critical reviews and certain other non-commercial uses permitted by copyright law.

MAISIE BARRETT

Printed Worldwide
First Printing 2023
First Edition 2023

10 9 8 7 6 5 4 3 2 1

"If you haven't confidence in self, you are twice defeated in the race of life."

Marcus Garvey (1887 – 1940)

Dedication

I dedicate this book to my dear, late mother, who helped get me out of an SEN school. I am grateful that she was my mother. Not forgetting my father, who gave me a sense of identity. He made me aware of African history and, although he was not aware of it, helped me appreciate my melanin skin, at a time when the world perceived Black Skin as ugly.

I thank the late father of my children for inviting me to Africa, where I decided the time had come for me to learn to read and write and educate myself and tell my story one day.

This book is also dedicated to Professor Robert Beckford, who encouraged me to write my story during the COVID-19 pandemic, when my autistic daughter went missing several times.

My book is also dedicated to all those who have shared their stories with the world. By doing so, they have helped shed light on what can happen in the life of an individual and behind closed doors (as Prince Harry declared), helped themselves and others heal and helped educate and change our complex world.

Watching True Stories has helped me in not focusing on my problems throughout these years. They have helped me think and cry for others instead of myself, to understand the Universe and the part I came to play in it.

Therefore, I hope my story and the message in this book will help someone heal through encouraging them to talk to someone or write about their experiences: we are not alone in our sufferings.

I further dedicate this book to London Metropolitan University for opening its doors to someone like me. I did all my degrees at London Met, which helped change my life.

I dedicate this book also to Marjorie Coley, in recognition of all her support after the death of my mother and for introducing me to a job that I love, supporting student social workers at London Met. Over the years, several social workers have been assigned to my family, so to find myself supporting them with their learning, to give them an opportunity to become the best social workers in England, is a gift from the Universe.

Last, but not least, I dedicate this book to my beloved grandson Malachi, my children (Noami, Kalunda and N'Kole) and my goddaughter Maisie.

Acknowledgement

I am exceedingly grateful to the Honourable Bernard Coard for creating awareness of how the British education system (that we now call a British scandal) treated black children in the '60s and '70s, when he wrote the book "How the West Indian Child Is Made Educationally Sub-normal in the British School System".

Bernard Coard laid down the foundation upon which Steve McQueen (Executive Producer) could produce the documentary, "Subnormal: A British Scandal", which resurrected the scandal that very few people knew about.

I cannot be more grateful that Lyttanya Shannon was chosen to produce and direct the documentary and for her kindness towards me throughout the filming of it. There were other Executive Producers and Producers I never had the pleasure of meeting, without whose expertise it would not have been possible to make the documentary. For example, Helen Bart, James Rogan, Soleta Rogan, Tracey Scoffield, Simon Barker and Esther Gimenez. Companies such as Rogan Productions, Lammas Park and Turbine Studios also made the documentary possible.

Were it not for my lovely friend Dr Juanita Cox Westmaas (whom I met at university), I would not have known about the documentary. Therefore, I cannot thank her enough for telling me about it and advising me to contact the Assistant Producer, Beya Kabelu, who interviewed me and concluded that my story should be included. Thank you, Beya.

Lastly, I would like to thank Martin Smith, who did a great deal of the editing of this book, and also Frances Swaine, from Leigh Day Solicitors, who contributed to editing this book. Leigh Day will endeavour to help me claim compensation from those responsible for placing me in an ESN school just because I was a black child. Noel Gardon, who was in the documentary with me, referred me to Leigh Day Solicitors. Thank you, Noel! And thank you, Jacinth Martin, for sending my details to Dave Neita, who is a barrister and was a Consultant at Leigh Day. So, it is fate that Leigh Day and I were to connect at some point.

You may well ask, why have I mentioned all these beautiful people? Well, without them, in chronological order starting with Bernard Coard, my book would be incomplete and have many missing pages. Therefore, I am forever indebted to them all.

Table of Contents

Leigh Day Solicitors 1
PART I 3
Foreword 5
Preface 11
Preface to Chapters 15
    One -Eight
        Chapter One 15
        Chapter Two 15
        Chapter Three 16
        Chapter Four 17
        Chapter Five 20
        Chapter Six 20
        Chapter Seven 21
        Chapter Eight 22
Introduction 25
Chapter One 27
    The Stone
Chapter Two 39
    Our Journey to The First Motherland
Chapter Three 69
    My Return to the Motherland (30 Years Later)
Chapter Four 77
    It Takes a Whole Village to Raise a Child: (My English Racist Teachers)

Chapter Five 99
    It Takes a Whole Village to Raise a Child: (My Colonial Family)

Chapter Six 123
    Meeting My Soul-Friend and My Soulmate And Going to College

Chapter Seven 149
    How I Failed my Children
    Because The British Education System Failed Me

Chapter Eight 203
    The Conclusion The Beginning

PART II **217**
    The Letters
    Dear African Leaders
    A United Africa Is The Future
    Start Trading With Each Other More

Bibliography 257
End Notes 259

Leigh Day Solicitors

During the 60s and 70s, black children of African-Caribbean heritage were subject to considerable discrimination in the way their school education was delivered.

Among other decisions taken, they were disproportionately allocated to schools for the Educationally Subnormal (ESN) or placed in ESN streams or remedial classes in mainstream schooling, and therefore deprived of the opportunities available to other children of the same age. There is considerable evidence to show that some of the reasons for these misallocations were due to Caribbean accents being unacceptable in the classroom; supremely low expectations of any child of African Caribbean heritage; and intentional and obvious cultural bias in generic school tests categorising which children were placed.

Schools and remedial streams originally set up following the 1944 Education Act, or those children needing to be cared for because of their special needs as a result of severe illness, or mental or physical disabilities, were used as a method of keeping many intelligent and physically able African

Caribbean children uneducated. In many cases, it is clear that this was because they were not expected to do more in life than move into those jobs which require little literacy or numeracy.

Maisie, the author of this book, had to leave school at 16, unable to read or write and therefore unable to function in society. She had no language to discuss any issues arising in her life. Her education had been in classrooms with no teaching at all, she was simply contained there with other children who often had severe disabilities, where any teaching was focused on ensuring their physical safety. The fact that Maisie eventually learnt to read and write properly in her 30s and today has four degrees, including a master's degree, has written her autobiography and a musical play about the Windrush children, does not mean that the suffering she has endured over the past five decades is in any way diminished On the contrary, it proves that she did not belong in a school for the Educationally Subnormal, where a child's IQ was supposed to be below 75.

The outcome for many of these children was a profoundly unhappy life. Aside from being formally uneducated, they were made to feel ignorant and self-esteem was, and often has remained, very low. All these things affected later life. Today, there is a large number of adults who were treated in this way, and at Leigh Day we are highlighting how such cases arose, the fault of central government policy and the inadequacy of local education assessments. Luckily, many of the "children" misclassified at the time are able to adduce a lot of hard evidence about what happened to them, the central and local government policies in place which clearly show their intentions, and outcomes which demonstrate years of trauma directly linked to what happened in the classrooms at the time. The links are very clear and we shall report back on the case as it progresses.

Frances Swaine

Leigh Day Solicitors

Priory House

PART I

Foreword

In late February and early March of 2022, during the war in Ukraine, close to three million Ukrainians fled their homes to escape missiles, mortars, bombs of all kinds. Eventually, more than ten million would be displaced, as many as six million fleeing to neighbouring countries. So, too, did thousands of Africans and Asians, mostly Indians, who were students at various universities in Ukraine, as also a few dozen from the Caribbean. Like the Ukrainians, the Africans, Asians, and Caribbeans travelled by car, bus, and train, whatever was available, to get to the Ukrainian border. However, unlike the Ukrainians, the African, Asian, and Caribbean people were ordered off of the buses and trains by Ukrainian police and border guards before they reached the border. Many were told openly that they were being ordered off because they were Black or Brown. This was not done to anyone who was white---including the white spouses of some of the students. These students therefore had to complete the journey to the border on foot; often walking for many hours, some for longer than one day. On reaching the closest border for most refugees, namely that with Poland, the Ukrainians were welcomed with open arms, hot drinks, food, and even blankets in some cases, and transport was provided to take them to accommodations in various locations for their safety and comfort. The Blacks and Browns were denied entry.

The governments of all these countries of the "South" were obliged to take urgent and energetic steps through their foreign ministries and ambassadors in Poland, Ukraine, and the other neighbouring, unwelcome States, in order to get the officials of these States to change the behaviour of their officials at the various borders. Thanks to technological advances and in particular modern cell phones, literally hundreds of videos of the above incidents were filmed and streamed, many in real time via the internet, to the watching world. This is what made it possible for affected governments to have indisputable evidence of what was happening, and for them to act swiftly to prevent possible catastrophe among their citizens being stranded without food, water, and appropriate clothing for any length of time, in open country, in an Eastern European winter. Without the evidence seen by people worldwide, there would have been blanket denials that any of this had indeed occurred. Indeed, the vast majority of the Western media gathered at the border chose not to report what their eyes had seen, repeatedly, over several days. They focused all their attention on the genuine plight of the citizens of Ukraine... Many of these white journalists carried stories in which they decried the fact that the devastation of war was happening in Europe. More than one noted that such things happened "in places like Africa and the Middle East"; not in "civilized countries in Europe". What has any of the above got to do with the extraordinary, first-person account, in this small but powerfully moving and ultimately uplifting book? What does the trauma of Black and Brown people at the Ukrainian/Polish border, in 2022, have to do with what happened to a little child of Caribbean parentage-the author of this book-who was packed off to a school for "Educationally Subnormal" children nearly sixty years ago? The answer is nothing, and everything. While the war in Ukraine was exactly three months and one day old, namely on May

25th, 2022, tens of thousands of people in the United States, Britain, Europe, and throughout Africa, Asia and the Caribbean, were marking the second anniversary of "lynchings" over many decades, and still unfolding, every year. Just days before that commemoration, there had been the mass killing of Black people in Buffalo, New York, by an eighteen-year-old white supremacist who streamed his murderous rampage live, and posted a "manifesto" justifying what he had just done...This was just the latest in such white supremacist mass killings of recent years...

Again, some readers may wish to know what is the relevance of lynching and mass murders of Black people in America to the packing off of large numbers of Black Caribbean children in the 1960's and 1970's in Britain, including the author of this book, Maisie Barrett, to schools where their spirits would be broken, their self-image, self-confidence, self-belief shattered; their career prospects permanently destroyed through deliberately denying them any meaningful education? The truth is, these and millions of other manifestations of oppression, subjugation, exploitation, discrimination over the past five hundred years, can be traced to an original virus, one which was and remains to this day global, hence it can be properly categorized as a pandemic. Starting with chattel slavery of African peoples, combined with the genocide of indigenous inhabitants of North, Central and South America, large swathes of Africa, and Australasia, then colonial rule throughout, including on the Asian continent; these developments of ruthless barbarism in the pursuit of ever more wealth, gave birth to this virus, this pandemic known as racism. Global in scale, this inhumanity had to be rationalized. The enslaved were not really human, but SUB: -human; inferior beings to the barbarians brutalizing them for their enrichment. Through 500 years of incubation and mutations, this racial virus has manifested itself in a wide variety of forms: in white civilian mob lynching, to police death squads, to the non-education and mis-education of Black children ---note, from being seen as SUB-human, to being placed in large numbers in schools for the SUB-normal---, to the murder and police cover up of the Stephen Lawrences of this world, and to the recent outrageous treatment of "Child Q" (and others the public has never even heard of in Britain); to the passing of laws in Britain to effectively criminalize Black and Brown refugees – and any who might provide humanitarian assistance to them-- fleeing persecution in countries in the global "South" (often a product of economic sanctions, bombings, and invasions by countries of the "North"); to the public welcome and financial assistance to fleeing Ukrainian refugees, while arranging to deport Black and Brown refugees to a country in Africa that they have never seen... What is outstanding about this book by Maisie Barrett, is its uplifting quality. It is fundamentally a story of extraordinary triumph over incredible adversity. It is the personal testimony of someone dispatched to a "dustbin" school as a child despite being of normal, indeed gifted intelligence. This true story is one of resilience, of determination to rise despite being pushed down; of deciding at age thirty that she just had to learn to read and write for herself, so that she could and would write her story, this book, for herself... Yes, Maisie recounts all the challenges, the travails; the fact that what was done to her by a callous, racist education system has had, in turn, profoundly negative consequences for her children, and for her grandchild Racism breeds generational curses, and Maisie continues, to this day, to struggle to defeat this curse as it has affected her children and grandchild. Maisie was one of only three individuals of Caribbean heritage who were placed in these many schools for the "Educationally Subnormal" half a century and more ago, who agreed to be interviewed on camera for the 2021 BBC 1 programme, "Subnormal", produced by Steve McQueen and co-produced and directed by Lyttanya Shannon. Others were frank in telling the producers that they were still, after all these years, ashamed to have been placed in these schools and therefore declined to be interviewed. One man agreed to explain, off camera and with his voice disguised, the fact that the stigma remains so great, that even today, he still had not told his wife that he had been placed in one of these schools.

This is why we must celebrate Maisie's courage, and her self-made accomplishments. This is why this book is inspirational, for Maisie's courage and determination, and her achievements against all the odds, gives all of us encouragement, a belief that we too can conquer disadvantage, discrimination, adversity in all its forms, and this is especially true when we tap into and leverage the social capital in our communities, organize ourselves as a people and form alliances such that we can defeat this virus. Racism is first and foremost an expression of the balance of forces or power between and among different races. No number of speeches, conferences, anti-racist education, and publications can by themselves defeat this pandemic. Only a change in the power relations will, ultimately do this. Black and Brown people, and the exploited white working class can and will defeat this virus by organizing to fundamentally alter the balance of power within the society. Until this is achieved, the virus will continue to wreak havoc in the lives of many if left unchecked. The good news is that the balance of power can be altered, racism can be defeated.

For this, courage, resilience, and a fighting, never give- up spirit are essential qualities. Maisie Barrett has shown us what is possible on all these fronts. Combined with Community Social Capital and alliances with others, victory can be achieved.

Copyright Bernard Coard (2022)

Preface

The book is written in an informal language while the second part is formal. In part one, I am trying to create a relaxing scene, as though I am narrating my story to you while we sit together in my living room.

Like all memories, the style of writing is reflective. Therefore, I go back and forward in time in order to tell my story, in my own dyslexic way, so please bear with me as you follow me on my life's journey.

No part of this narrative is fictitious or exaggerated. It is told according to my experiences and memory, and it is the truth. I have not revealed where I was brought up in England or the country I went to live in in Africa. However, I can say that I was born in Birmingham, England to Jamaican parents and I now live in London.

I've made a great effort not to disclose any personal accounts of other people's lives without their consent but I will write about how they influenced my life, and why, without their consent. In addition, I am not writing out of anger, resentment, or spitefulness. I just want to tell my story because I promised myself I would, at a time when I was in great despair and a very long way from home.

First, let me explain how the title 'Subnormal: How I was Failed by the British Education System and a Colonial Family' came to mind. In the '60s, I went to a special needs school (ESN), where I was made educationally subnormal. They designed these schools for children who could not learn. I went to this school when I was about six years old, and I left at thirteen, when I went to a mainstream school.

My parents came to England in the '50s. Like most West Indians, they came with high expectations as a black English couple. My mother specifically believed the way of life of the natives of England, and their white skin, were superior to those of Caribbean people. My father was more aware of his African roots and history, but he still possessed elements of colonial conditioning, especially in the home.

Therefore, when I say 'colonial parents', I mean my parents derived from an epoch that had not long ago overcome enslavement but my parents were nevertheless still living their lives and being educated in a way that had been started by the colonisers who had enslaved them. And so, they came to Britain with a colonial mindset. They were taught by the colonisers that England was the mother country, and they believed this. England was so great they coined the phrase that England's 'streets were paved with gold', as though it was heaven, but while few experienced heaven in England back then, many went through hell to even find a place to live.

When West Indians first arrived in England, they didn't see themselves as strangers – therefore, they were confident that they would be treated the same as the natives of England, and their children would be educated the same as the next English child. Some parents realised that back home the education was superior to the education in England, and sent their children home for education, while my parents trusted the British education system. Therefore, when I went to a special school my parents were confident that the teachers would give me special attention.

I went to university in the year 2000, and I told a student with whom I became very good friends that I attended an SEN school. Twenty years later, she contacted me on Facebook, asking me if I would like to feature in a documentary called 'Subnormal: A British scandal'. The documentary coverage was about black children being placed in SEN schools just because they were black. It didn't matter if these children were intelligent.

All my life I was ambivalent about what Special Educational Needs really meant and the impact it had on my life, personality, and how I interact with people in the past and now. Until the documentary in 2020, I didn't even know I had had a subnormal education. I began writing my book not knowing that there were more pages to my book.

In addition to the above, I was convinced that being dyslexic was the cause of most of my problems. However, the reality was that I was really suffering from a man-made disability; a semi-retardation condition that they chose for me to have, not because I was a slow learner, but because I was a black child. How unlucky was I?

The bad luck element is that going to an ESN school did not prepare me for life's diversities and conflicts and allow me to make a positive difference in my life and in society. I was put into a clever, evil, racist system that worked like a CHAIN OF REACTION to ensure that not only I would not amount to anything important in society, but neither would my children and grandchildren. Before I die, I will break that CHAIN.

Preface to Chapters
One - Eight

Chapter One
The Stone

In this chapter, you will see how the diversity I mentioned previously helped the fact dawn on me that the time had come and that, no matter what, I was going to learn to read and write properly and tell my story to the world one day. I bring you to that very point thirty years ago, when I arrived at the most frustrating moment in my life. I wanted to write what I was going through at the time, and I just couldn't. My relationship with my fiancé came to a sudden end while I was in Africa, and I couldn't afford to return home with my three children. When I tried to write a letter to my mother, I remember saying, "Oh, my God, I can't do this. I can't find the words to explain and express myself". I thought out loud that what I was going through at that time "was all bigger than myself".

Chapter Two
Our Journey to the Motherland

As a Caribbean British-born, this chapter goes back in time to show how I came to be in Africa in the first place, when I had an argument with my fiancé. In the '70s, when I was a teenager, it was a time when Africans from around the world grew their Afro hair as big as they could, and many black musicians sang songs about going back to Africa. While watching the television in my parents' bedroom, because the living room was rented out to a Windrush migrant, my father would entertain his friends, and he often talked about African history. I was always fascinated by these stories. When I was about fifteen years old, I had a dream that I went to Africa and walked on the greenest grass I had ever seen. In the dream, I remember feeling completely tranquil and safe. It wasn't always my dream to marry an African man and go to Africa to live, but I became obsessed with the idea when, in my early twenties, I moved to London where there was a large African community.

The first sentence in this chapter begins "At last, the moment came when I knew my children and I were about to go to Africa". I couldn't believe it was actually happening! You will see how excited I was to be going to Africa to be with the man I loved who I would marry. But you will also see, unlike my dream of walking on the greenest grass in the most tranquil atmosphere, that my experience was destined to be the opposite.

Chapter Three

My return to the Motherland

In this chapter, I take you back to Africa to the funeral of the man I once used to call my soulmate, the father of my boys and stepfather to my daughter. In truth, although it was not meant for us to be together, he was still a very significant figure in my life who helped me evolve and move me towards my destiny.

It was in his homeland that I decided to learn to read and write properly and educate myself in order to tell my story one day.

Again, it was in his homeland, thirty years later when I went to his funeral, that I had a strong urge to write a political letter to the leaders of Africa, encouraging them to unite and find a remedy for the socio-economic and political problems in Africa, bearing in mind that, thirty years ago, I couldn't even write a letter to my mother!

Chapter Four
It Takes a Whole Village to Raise a Child: (My Racist British Teachers)

The premise of the title of this chapter is self-explanatory. It clearly shows that society, as a whole, is also responsible for the safety, development and prosperity of a child, while the family is a part of society that plays an imperative part, too. However, society plays a greater part in your child's development than you think. I am referring to the education industry, where children spend more of their active time in school before going to college and university. This could be why some parents teach their children at home, but they still have to live and further develop in society, which can take them down another pathway that makes the parents ask, "Where did we go wrong?".

And thus, this chapter tells the story of how I was deliberately (because I was a black child) placed in an ESN school, to prevent me from climbing the social ladder. The British Government invited Caribbean people to England to help rebuild the economy after the Second World War; and they happily left their homes and families to help Britain, although their countries were also affected by the war. The British Government repaid them by sending their children to special needs schools.

My parents came from a society in the Caribbean framed on the foundation of African traditions, where a neighbour, a complete stranger, or even a teacher, often watched out for the children in the community. Any adult could discipline a child who was not behaving on the streets. In addition, after hundreds of years of enslavement, children's education was the most important thing in Caribbean society and they were educated to the highest level, especially if they were from a certain class, like my mother.

My mother told me that her father boarded out his youngest daughter to live with an aristocrat English schoolmistress when he received a lump sum of money from his insurance policy. company, he boarded out his youngest daughter to live with an aristocrat English schoolmistress to be educated, in order to have the best education and speak the queen's language like the aristocrats. When my young aunt arrived in England in the early '50s, she became a Ward Sister within a short space of time. My grandfather also helped my mother start a business after she left school; teaching dressmaking, tailoring, crochet and knitting to young girls and ladies.

As a matter of fact, my mother didn't really need to come to England at all, because she derived from the 'coloured class' and had the very best of education; she came to be with her husband. Before going any further, let me explain coloured class. During slavery, according to historical accounts, a new class of people was emerging throughout the Americas. Slave traders began raping enslaved African women on the ships and continued to do so when they arrived on the 'slave land'. The children of these raped enslaved African women were immediately seen as superior to the Africans, especially the freshly arrived slaves who were very dark-skinned. Even through colonial times, people of mixed-race, with light skin, or those who could pass for white, were seen as superior and often became political leaders of their countries after independence.

Going back to education, and on how important it was in my mother's family, in the Caribbean, although my mother wasn't taught about African history, culture and traditions, she had a good education and was very good at English and Maths. She told me her father was a Mathematician and used to help her with her Maths. She used to recite English poems and nursery rhymes to me, although not as often as I would have liked. In addition, she had beautiful handwriting that gradually deteriorated with age. Apparently, her twin sister was brighter than her, which means she was well-educated, and her intelligence quotient was above average.

My mother wanted me to have an excellent education, and to affirm her heart's desire in the Universe, she named me after one of her peers at school, who always passed her exams and grew up to become a teacher.

When my parents came to Britain, they believed England was the mother country. They were brainwashed into believing that British culture, traditions, mentality, morals and, most significantly, their education system, were superior to theirs; after all, my mother told me that their teachers sent exam papers to be marked in England. Therefore, if British people could mark exams for these teachers, and give them fair marks, why wouldn't they teach their children as they do their own?

Chapter Five

It Takes a Whole Village to Raise a Child: (My Colonial Family).

This chapter shows that while I was being made educationally subnormal by the British system I was also very unhappy at home, living with parents who had come from a different world. I was a child, so I was supposed to be seen and not heard and mother and I often experienced my father anger with his hand or a hard object.

One day, my mother told me that I was going to live with my aunt, and I was so happy. My aunt used to come with her husband and daughter to visit us, and they seemed like a perfect family. You know what it is like; the grass is always greener on the other side until one day you decide to go over there, and you realise that it's worse than yours. I soon realised that ghostly toxic home was a better place to live than my aunt's house, and it became my heart's desire to return home; unknowingly, I wished for something, and it happened.

Chapter Six

Meeting My Soul-Friend and Soulmate and Going to College for The First Time.

This chapter takes you to the moment when I met my soul-friend and through my soul-friend, unknowingly to her at that time, I would meet my soulmate, the father of my boys. Also, with her encouragement, I went to college for the first time. This chapter takes you to the time when I met them both in the space of eight years, and how they helped change my life and move me towards my destiny.

Chapter Seven

How I Failed My Children Because the British Education System Failed Me First

I do not blame all my family's problems on the fact that I went to an SEN school, but it surely helped to make my family's life 'subnormal' (dysfunctional). In this instance, when I say family, I am referring to my children.

This was the hardest chapter to write. When I was writing it, halfway through, I just couldn't deal with my emotions and, for three months, I couldn't write; it was hard to structure this chapter because of this. When I began writing again, I had to face and deal with my emotions over and over again every time I edited the manuscript.

In this chapter, I share with you my story of when I arrived back home in England from Africa and realised that I was a single parent and going to raise my children alone. It was important to me to raise them in a nuclear family with both parents. My mother and all her sisters were married, even my father's daughters were married. I really believed that I had failed my children because I was an uneducated mother; I became very depressed and allowed loneliness to affect me in every way.

At that time, I had almost zero confidence and self-esteem. I lacked certain social skills because I went to an SEN school and could not provide the stability and the home my dear children deserved, like all children do.

My struggle to be a single mother was made worse when I noticed that my two eldest had extra needs, but sadly, I was on a mission to educate myself, and I knew it wouldn't be easy because I found learning really very difficult. The reason for this is that they did not teach me to learn at school. My brain was like a body that had never exercised, like feral children who are raised by dogs will bark and also use their hands to walk like a dog because this is what their brain has been trained to tell their bodies to do. The day I left the mainstream school to go to the special school, my brain stopped being stimulated. As the years went by, I behaved immature for my age and could not read or write.

When I returned to school at 32, I needed more and more time to learn basic English and Maths in order to go on to further my education and I couldn't work and study at the same time to give my children a better quality of life. I took that time at their expense, for this reason, I failed to meet their needs, as their mother, and this backfired, causing a crippling devastating effect but not one that cannot be rectified. We are healing! Once there is life, there will be a road before us that will lead us to our true destiny.

Chapter Eight
The Conclusion! The Beginning!

Fortunately, the great thing about humans is the ability to evolve. I am glad to declare in this part of the narrative that I have evolved and will continue to do so with the help of the Universe that I believe God created for our use.

It is my opinion that we are living in a time of enlightenment that is different to the Enlightenment that emerged throughout Europe from the late 17th to the early 19th centuries that witnessed the deadly contagious birth of racism, used as an excuse for continue for slavery.

The enlightenment I am referring to here is the enlightenment that arose throughout the beginning of creation when people had a greater understanding of spirituality. They knew how to manipulate the Universe to attract or manifest what they wanted and to improve or heal themselves. This great ability was replaced with religion by the very people who now practise African spirituality. They call it 'the law of attraction', after researching, reshaping, and renaming it to suit themselves. This took place in the 1500s, during the early years of the European Transatlantic Slave Trade, when Europeans discovered African spirituality before it became associated with negative connotations, such as black magic and voodoo.

Our experiences in life, whether they be positive or negative, should help us become our better selves if we sustain a cheerful outlook on life and abstain from fury and retribution, and so on. Thinking positive is the basic fundamental principle of African spirituality. I am more spiritual than ever before as I continue to develop into my greater self, and I hope and pray that my children and their offspring will do too.

Introduction

I started the narration of this book at the age of nearly 30. At this age, Mother Nature was about to throw me from the cradle – like the way eagles prepare their young to find food and defend themselves. Every day, the eagle flies and brings food for its little eaglets until, one day, it comes back with nothing for them to eat. Instead, one by one, she flies high in the sky and drops them. She does this several times until they can fly independently to find food for themselves among their many predators, who would be happy to devour them, like the mighty hurricane of the earth. What I mean by this metaphor is that we are often the prey of nature. Everything has its prey which it feeds off, including humans.

You may say that nearly 30 years old is a mature age; yes, for some. Each individual has their own lessons to learn in this life according to their past-life experiences (if you believe in reincarnation like I do), their own abilities, talents and earthly background, which includes parents and the society in which they grow and live.

There were no warnings, and I was not prepared. I thought I was a grown woman, with three young children, but what I experienced when I went to live in Africa made me realise that I was just a spoiled British girl fashioned to think and behave in a certain way by British society and my family.

But now, I was going to be taught life's lessons in order to develop into the woman I should have been (at that time) and who I MUST become before the predators of British society got hold of me; and what better place to mature than in Africa, the birthplace of humanity.

CHAPTER ONE
THE STONE

It was during one of those quarrels that I realised that it would be the last one, after months of contempt for one another, and just sheer fury and resentment, whenever we were in the same room. I may not have had a great command of the English language, due to having a limited vocabulary as a dyslexic adult, and wasn't taught English language and grammar at school, but I had the words to argue with great range, like anyone would who is very angry and very disappointed with someone.

I realised that he was in a relationship with two women, one of whom was pregnant, and his greatest desire was to see the back of me, even though I had given up my home in England to travel with our children to Africa in order to be with him. We were going to get married and my mother was making the wedding dress in England. I couldn't believe what I was experiencing. We were only apart from each for just over a year, but by the time the children and I joined him, he had changed towards me, for the worse.

He yelled out frantically, "I have always been like this. I had an affair with…" and he called out the name of my soul-friend, whom I loved and saw as my sister, but my sister would never allow me to be with a man she knew was unfaithful and did not love me. Now, I knew why she wasn't happy for me when we got engaged, and why she didn't even bother to come with me to the airport when I was travelling to be with him in Africa.

Then, there was a sudden silence because I needed time to record in my mind what he had just told me about having an affair with her. He looked down to his feet in shock that he had confessed his deceitful, evil actions without planning it, before attempting to get off the bed and leave the room. But I made him look up again, when I furiously uttered words of great anger and disappointment, in my then world of emptiness, despair and pain. He was my soulmate, and she was my soul-friend, and I have never ceased to love them both until this very day.

Thereafter, no words I flung at him could have revealed how angry and disappointed I was with him. Only one gesture could have symbolised how I undoubtedly felt. It was at that point that our relationship came to a sudden end, which was not my true intention. I wanted us to be together, although I had always had my doubts because of the dream I had had. I tempestuously forced the engagement ring off my finger and flung it across the room, aiming for his head. I thought he would have picked it up, lovingly thrown his arms around me and apologised. But instead, breathing heavily with protruding lips, he bent down and grabbed the ring from the floor, as though he had snatched it from someone's hand in great fury. He then attempted to throw it back at me, when suddenly he turned, walked towards the window, opened it, and threw it out. With his eyes fixed on the door, he swiftly walked past me, as though I was a ghost, opened the door, and triumphantly walked out of the room, slamming it loudly behind him. The children and I didn't see him for days after that.

Then suddenly the room was filled with only my heart beating away loudly, until there was silence when I had calmed down. I don't know how long I had been standing there, just looking, when his face appeared in my mind's eye. I went over to the wardrobe and pulled out a bag with photos in it and searched eagerly for his pictures. I tore them up. Then the face of my soul-friend appeared before me and I searched for her pictures, too, before shredding them into tiny pieces.

Convinced that both of them were a bad omen in my life, I threw the ripped-up photos out of the window together with the stone the fortune-teller had given me. Then I started sobbing uncontrollably for so many reasons. It wasn't just because of a broken heart; it was because of my entire life up to that point. I used to compare my life to a having pure heavenly gold in my hands that disappeared when I open it. I truly believed that is how unlucky I was.

I stopped crying to write a letter to my mother to tell her that my life was a living hell, and that the man I had travelled so far to be with didn't love me any more; if he had ever loved at all. I wanted to ask her to raise the money for my three children and I to return to England, but when I tried writing it down, I couldn't find the words to describe the horror I was going through, because I could hardly read or write and my vocabulary was very small.

I became frustrated and discouraged, so I put the paper and pen on the bed and walked sadly over to the corner of the room and sat there with my legs crossed and cried and cried. I cried until it rained and thundered with lightning. In Africa, when it rained, it reminded me of a verse in the Bible that describes the end of the world. It thundered as if the heavens were about to open. For a moment, I felt as though it was the end of my world.

It was already evening, so it didn't take long before the sky turned to black, and the full moon stood strong amid a few scattered stars. All this time, I must have been looking into the sky, because I had not noticed that I had cried a tiny pool of tears on the floor in front of me. With a heavy hand, I wrote my initials in my tears, as I pleaded with God to help me. I had convinced myself that I didn't have a brain, so I promised God that if he helped me to dig myself out of this dark pit I had sunk deeper and deeper into, I would get my brain working like everyone else and tell the world my story. I suddenly gained some strength.

I really believed in my conviction that God was going to help me return home to England, a country I never thought I belonged to because of my African-Caribbean heritage and the racism there. I always wanted to live in a black country. But I was born and bred in England, and I had a feeling, at the time, that I wouldn't develop into the woman I was born to be if I didn't return home. Although I knew this, I still couldn't let go of my dream of living in Africa.

Once my fiancé had finished studying law in Europe and returned to Africa, we spoke endlessly on the phone about how I would contribute to helping the family financially when the children and I joined him. The plan was that I would study hairdressing, and we would open up a salon in Africa, but neither of us thought about the theoretical side of hairdressing, only the practical side of it. Thinking about it now, perhaps he would have arranged for someone to teach me in Africa, so I wouldn't have to study the theory.

THE STONE

In 1987, not long after I gave birth in November, my fiancé travelled back home to Africa, either at the end of that year or the beginning of 1988. I can't remember the exact time. The plan was that the children and I would follow him within a year, and we would marry. While he was preparing for us, I paid to do a hairdressing course because I didn't want to wait to go to Africa to study there. I wanted to surprise him, to make him proud. The course was perfect. It was private, so I didn't have to enrol, and I didn't have to do written exams. It was basically a tick-box exam and a lot of practical assignments, which I almost failed, but I managed to pass.

I graduated from hairdressing in March 1989 and I travelled to Africa in April, but before I travelled, an Indian man,(fortune-teller) who could predict the future rang the doorbell. It wasn't the first time he had come, but I always sent him away because I was a Christian, and the Bible teaches that having your future told is a sin. But this time I allowed him to come inside because I was going to live in Africa and I wanted to know if I would live 'happily ever after' as I always had a strange feeling I wouldn't, but I still had to go.

The reason I needed to know the future was because, in 1983, I had dreamt that bugs were all over me. They were strange creatures, I had never seen before and I knew they were from another country or even another world. Even more strange, I awoke from the dream, and I had a weird feeling that the dream was connected to my fiancé, who was laying next to me in the bed. Therefore, I thought that allowing the Indian man inside my house would be a good opportunity to ask him to interpret the dream. I knew in my heart that nothing he could say would have stopped me from going to Africa, but I just needed to know the future.

When he came inside the house, I told him that I had a bad feeling about going to Africa, and I told him the dream. He looked deep into my eyes and asked me to choose a number between 1 and 5, and I chose 3. Subconsciously, I don't know why I chose this number. Could it be that the family house I lived in with my parents was number 3? Coincidently, I was 3 years old when my father bought the house and we went to live there. When my mother took her last breath, the time was 3:33 in the afternoon. The number 3 continues to appear in my life.

The Indian man gave me a shiny black stone that I discovered years later had the Hindu Goddess Vishnu carved into it. It was the first time I had seen this, so I thought at the time it was a lucky charm, but I always called it 'the stone'. He placed the stone in the palm of my hand and told me not to say anything to anyone, or even tell anyone my dreams, but as soon as my mother entered the room, I told her. Immediately after I had told her, I saw the disappointment on the her face, but I didn't see my mother as being just anyone, and so I forgot. I knew I had done something wrong, and I was worried that I had cursed myself because I had disobeyed the Indian man.

Now I had a double bad feeling, about the dream and disobeying the Indian man. It later became a triple bad feeling. That night, I dreamt that someone related to my fiancé bit off one of my nipples. Disobeying the Indian man again, I told my mother, and she said it was a bad dream. Originating from a superstitious time and culture, a bad dream to my mother signified bad things would happen. Today, I don't believe in superstitions. Anyway, during that time I did, and I just couldn't keep my mouth shut. And I am still doing it now, as I share my story with you.

When we open our mouth to speak, words leave our lips and linger in the air, doing either good or harm. That is why, in virtually every culture, there are proverbs about the tongue and how we should try to control it by saying less. In my parents' country, there is a proverb that goes, "a nuh everything good fe eat good fi taak". The translation is: "It's not everything that is good to eat is good to be talked about". "The wise person has long ears and short tongue", say American Indians. The fathers of the Bible also recognised the power of the tongue. I have chosen one quote among many out of the Bible, to help push my story along. In Proverbs 12: 18-19 it teaches us that "The words of the reckless tongue pierce like swords, but the tongue of the wise brings healing".

When I disobeyed the fortune-teller, did I send words into the air that would return in a thousand piercing swords to destroy and torment me and my beloved children? Many people would answer yes to this question, while others may disagree. I will leave you to be the judge as you read on. Roland Barthes teaches us that "The birth of the reader must be required by the death of the author". Therefore, I must give you the space to interpret according to your own beliefs.

I was conscious that I would do better at my own business than to work for someone else and, over the years, I have established this view, even up to the present. Sadly, I never gained the skills necessary to thrive in society, but only to survive. Therefore, from the onset, I have always wanted to set up a business because I didn't have the social skills to work with others in a team. At one time, I tried to learn to make jewellery and bags, but I lacked the confidence and self-esteem to network and sell. Afterwards, I bought a knitting machine, but nothing came out of that idea. Finally, I decided to learn hairdressing. I joined my aunty's pardner, which is a saving system whereby we all save as a group and each week or month one person collects the savings, but continues to pay until the last one collects their money. When it was my turn to collect my savings, I enrolled in a hairdressing course. Despite the fact that most of the students fell out with me, I just managed to pass the course, because I didn't have to take any written exams. Before I went to Africa, I bought a professional hair dryer and steamer, a leather salon chair, a sofa for the salon and hair products. I worked at home, doing mostly washing, conditioning and hair extensions. I had completed different modules of the course in October, November and December 1988, in perming, cutting and blow drying, hair waving and weaving in 1989.

What I had learnt at college was slowly making sense, but I had a long way to go to gain experience and confidence. I wasn't that good at hairdressing, but what better place to learn than Africa, with the love and support I would have there, I asked myself back then?

My fiancé and I spoke every day on the phone. As far as I knew, he loved me. He always used to say he loved me more than I loved him. Although our relationship was often long-distance, we saw each other more than some couples who lived in the same country but in different homes. During the summer holidays, when he broke up from university, we either went to Europe with the children or he came to be with us in England. Sometimes, he would take his suitcase to university, travel to England on the Friday night, return on Monday morning and go straight to his lessons.

In my opinion, he treated me like a lady. When we were walking, he never allowed me to walk on the outside of the pavement, so he could protect me. He always allowed me to get on the bus first and sit down. At the bus stop, while waiting for a bus in the cold weather, he would wrap his coat around me and he would either whisper sweet things into my ear or sing to me. He had a singing voice like an angel, which my youngest child has inherited. He was gentle and very polite, with excellent manners and very intelligent.

During one of our many conversations when he was in Africa, I asked him to send me the measurements of the windows so I could buy the lace curtains for our home when I went to live there. He suggested I buy raw lace curtains to cut to the size of the windows because he didn't have time to measure windows. We were also planning a wedding; well at least I was. Mum and I bought the material for my wedding dress and the bridesmaid dresses. The plan was that she would make my wedding dress and join us in Africa because I had no intention of returning to England, not even to visit, after she had joined us. I used to say that the Queen of England would never see me again, so I threw away my coat, as a symbolic gesture.

Bringing up my children in Africa meant that, unlike me, they would have a real identity that is recognised because being black and British, in my opinion, meant nothing to the Queen of England and her politicians. At least in the Caribbean, once you are born in England, they see and treat you as an English person, whereas in England black people are still considered as foreigners, even if they are born here. When I was in Africa and I told them that I was Black British, they couldn't relate to it in the '80s. They asked me if I was African

American. In the end, I told them that I was West Indian, though I was born in England and had never been to the West Indies.

I wanted my children to live in a country where most of the people looked like them, and where there were role models they could look up to and respect. But most importantly, I wanted them to be educated in Africa and be multilingual like their father (who I thought was the most intelligent man I had ever met) and to return to England to further their education; but, that wasn't their destiny.

Like most parents, my children's future is very important to me.

Africa was the place where I wanted my children to grow up and be educated. I wanted them to be bilingual like most Africans.

But going to live there did nothing for them.

At the beginning of the story, I started with an argument my fiancé and I were having at the time. Now, I would like to share with you everything that led up to that argument.

Welcome, as I take you with me on the journey to the

Motherland Africa.

Chapter Two

Our Journey to The First Motherland

April 1989

At last, the moment came when our tickets were ready for us to travel to Africa. I was immensely excited. Knowing I would see my fiancé again was an overwhelming feeling but going to Mother Africa (for the first time) was equally profuse happiness, although I still had that weird feeling that something wasn't right because of the dream I had. Also, I was very worried about leaving my mother alone, even though I knew if anything should happen to me, her family would take care of her.

I checked in, and was about to enter the gate of no return, when I felt a powerful urge to turn around to take one last look at my mother's face before boarding the plane. I called this part of the journey "gate of no return" because I wasn't going to return to England. The expression on my mother's face was pure horror when I turned to look at her. In the Christian tradition, it is bad luck to 'look back' – like Lot's wife who turned into a pillar of salt when she disobeyed the angels for looking back at the evil city they were told to leave, before God destroyed the city and everything in it. That day, my poor mother must have gone home with her heart in her mouth (as they say in the Caribbean). I knew she was thinking the worst because of what I had done.

My heart swelled with grief and regret that I was so absent-minded and had forgotten this biblical myth, and how seriously people of my mother's generation took it. That intense scene never entered my mind again, until now, as I share my story with you. Thereafter a chain of bad omens occurred, and they were unstoppable.

Once we boarded, after tucking up my children in their seats, I took my place near the window as it flew up and up into the English spring sky. The sun was hidden behind the vast clouds that floated below the heavens, as the rain came pouring down on the windows. I remember thinking that I hoped there would not be a thunderstorm because I didn't want to be caught in a storm. Flying was certainly not my favourite activity. I tried to take my mind off the weather, by focusing on how my dream was at last coming to fruition – to go to Africa to marry the man together with whom I thought we would be successful in marriage and business.

During the flight, I was so impatient because the flight seemed to be taking forever. I had never flown that far before. We had to stop off in Belgium before boarding a second plane to take us to our glorious destination. The African air hostess greeted us, and it was the first time I had seen a black air hostess because I had not travelled to Africa or the Caribbean before.

We flew through many skies, from white and blue to black, but there was no sky like the African morning sky as the plane approached its ancient clouds; the land of the first man and woman. It was a great honour to be among my ancestors.

A huge, victorious smile extended across my heart, when I told my children "we are here now, we will see daddy soon". I placed my hand on my chest in amazement, as if I had just seen the clouds welcoming us with open arms. Joy swelled my soul, and it was running over like a stream with pure happiness. Although it was very early in the morning, it was warmer than the afternoon in England in summer when we descended from the plane. It was surprising, to me, how cool and sightly warm the air felt on my skin but this was a warning that the evening would be mighty hot.

I heard my name and looked up, but I couldn't see my fiancé. When I entered the airport, and saw the black portraits on the wall, it confirmed to me again that I was in the Motherland.

Suddenly, I was in the arms of my soulmate. Squeezing me tightly against his pounding heart, I could feel the eyes of his family peering at me curiously. He had tears in his eyes, but it must have been tears of regret. That peculiar, strange feeling from the night of the dream suddenly came over me, which I had not felt since I boarded the plane. The feeling was so strong, and somehow, strangely, I knew he was feeling it too. So, when we embraced, I felt a wedge between our beating hearts as our noses brushed against each other, like two swans meeting for the first time, although we had known each other for nearly six years. Before we left the airport, I had to put my signature on a document, and I was so embarrassed when my fiancé giggled with his family when I couldn't write my signature properly, but I put that image out of my mind very quickly. And to be honest, I only remembered it when I started to write this book.

I don't know if it was an African custom, but the first place we went after the airport was to my fiancé's grandmother's house. She was very old and frail, with beautiful dark and wrinkly, tough skin.

Her tiny bare feet came running towards us with her arms stretched out, to take my baby out of my arms. She lovingly kissed him, and he cried as he clinched onto me, refusing to go to her. She was so old that she even frightened my other two children. After his grandmother's house, we went to his workplace to meet his Arabian boss, whose wife was from Europe, before going to his office to meet his colleagues however, once we where there, I didn't say much, as usual.

That same day, we went to his mother's house where we met some of the family. His two brothers and their wives and children were there, and also his two sisters and their husbands and children, cousins and friends were all there. It was a full house! Only a few of his family spoke a little English, but even if they all spoke English, I still would have had little to say in those days, and I was too tired to talk, anyway.

It had been a long day because we arrived very early in the morning. The children were now fast asleep, and I couldn't stop my eyelids from closing from time to time. I was exhausted from the flight and overwhelmed to be in Africa. I had asked my fiancé several times when we were going home, but he kept telling me to wait. Also, I couldn't wait to see our house.

At last, the time had come for us to leave his mum's place. The baby remained sleeping in my arms, as my two eldest were half asleep and struggled to walk to the car. Before we got home, he stopped outside a hotel, which made me annoyed, but I was too tired to say anything, at first.

As if I was drunk, with a slurring voice I asked him, "why are we stopping here"?

"Are we going to live in a hotel?", I asked sarcastically, although I knew the answer had to be "no". But he didn't answer; he just looked at me and said, in a commanding voice, "Let's go inside. We will sleep here tonight" he said, in a cold and commanding voice.

In sheer disappointment, I asked, "Why? Isn't our place ready?".

"Let's go", he said, hastily.

Entering the hotel, I remember the reception being dark, although the light was on. The two men behind the reception desk greeted us in their language. When they realised I spoke English, they laughed and said hello in English, but that was all they could say. The other man directed us to our room. When the door opened, the first thing I saw was the window leading to a veranda. It was a small double-size room with a semi-double bed.

I tried to turn an odd situation into a normal one, by replacing it with the thought of us sleeping together as a family, after more than a year of being apart. But then that strange feeling came over me again – I was at war with its invisible presence. Determined to fight all the negativity that was invading my mind, I replaced it with the colourful, prosperous future that I had planned to build with my fiancé. I quickly opened the suitcase and proudly, with a radiant smile, I handed him my hairdressing certificates, eager to receive compliments, a hug or at least eye contact.

"Look", I said softly, in a childish way, calling him by his name, "I did it! You always said that I was intelligent and look, you were right".

"What is it?", he asked coldly, with a stern look on his face. It was obvious by the tone of his voice and his deep-set dark eyes that he was not interested at all in what I was about to tell him. As he looked uneasily towards the door, as though he wanted to leave, I said proudly, "I went to college to learn hairdressing and I am hoping we can open a salon together". I told him I had bought salon chairs, hair dryers, a steamer and hair products which would arrive next month. He took the certificates, looked at them without interest and, within seconds, he placed them on the bed and walked straight out of the door, saying "That's good", as he closed the door behind him; he spent no more than ten minutes with us, after not seeing me and the children for so long.

After bathing the children and getting them ready for bed, it occurred to me that perhaps he was downstairs in reception talking to the bar staff, but when I went there, he was nowhere to be seen. I was told that he went out and would not be returning. They told me in their language and somehow I understood them. I also had an inclination that they knew something I didn't know.

On his return the next morning, he drove us to his mother's house to eat, but he didn't stay to eat with us. He continued to drive us to his mother's place each day, until I could find my way there. There were no buses, and he didn't leave any money to take a taxi. I used to walk on hot sandy roads for a few miles to his mother's, just to eat and sit there depressed and alone in the sun, asking myself, what have I done, and was this was how I was going to live the rest of my life? I suddenly felt trapped in a world of sand. What hurt me the most was that months had gone by and still my precious children weren't going to school.

Every day, the children and I were getting skinnier and skinnier as we walked to their grandmother's house on an empty stomach under central Africa's scorching sun. Sometimes, I would send my five-year-old son to look for food when his little friends came to play with him; I also told my daughter this when two little girls came to knock for her to play out. I can't believe I did this. I must have known they would be safe. Looking back, I don't know how this was possible; it could not have happened in England. My children were unaware of the true reality of what was going on and even today, as adults, they have fun memories of Africa – that is the beauty of being a child! Whereas for me, the whole experience was becoming more and more like hell.

My fiancé didn't help towards our upkeep regularly. His mother was a widow who received a small pension because her husband was a politician and had died while he was working in Europe. So, she had a small business selling ground rice and cassava. This was what my fiancé had told me.

We'd argue and argue when he came to the hotel, or at his mum's house, because we rarely ever saw him. The bright light in the tunnel went out, and my dream was shattered. I felt like a silly, naïve goat, trapped in a lion's den that I had chosen to walk into.

At the end of the month, the family summoned a significant uncle to the house for a family meeting. Every month we had a family meeting. They would discuss all the family problems, but they left ours until last, because it was a very complicated problem that was hard to find a solution for. It was at that first meeting, we discovered, that he had not prepared a home for us because he was living with his pregnant girlfriend; the same lady he told me to greet and kiss twice on each cheek when she came to mum's house to meet me for the first time, when I had been unaware of who she was. I was unaware of who my fiancé was too, although we were together for six years and had two children. I didn't know that he had it in him to be unfaithful, spiteful and cold towards me.

When the family discovered the truth, they were ashamed and accused him of inviting me to Africa to take his children. We were all shocked at how irresponsible he was. At the end of the meeting, the children were sleeping and I was exhausted, not physically, but mentally. I just wanted to go back to the hotel. Yes, months had gone by, and we were still living at the hotel. My heart was on the floor, and he was stepping all over it and rubbing my nose into it. I just couldn't take my eyes off him. There was no shame on his face, but I could tell that he was frustrated. I guess he just didn't love me enough to spend the rest of his life with me. If I could have secretly killed him with my eyes, I would have done so and regretted it later.

After some time, we left the hotel to move to one with a larger and cheaper room. Each day, the children and I were getting more and more dehydrated. We also had ongoing diarrhoea for months, so much so that the laundry department in the hotel complained we were ruining the sheets.

One morning, I woke up to find my baby's belly as big as a nine-month pregnant woman, and sometimes when he woke up some of his hair had fallen onto the pillow. Unlike me, the children constantly got malaria. By now, I was finding my way around; I took them to the doctor and literally begged for malaria medicine because I didn't have money to pay for the treatment. The medicine was powder, which the doctor mixed with water in a tablespoon and gently forced it down their throats; they wouldn't have taken it otherwise because it was too bitter.

The staff became like family at this hotel. One of the bar staff spoke English, so I spoke to him all the time about everything. I used to pour out my heart to him. He often became quite emotional after talking to me. All the staff saw my pain and supported me the best way they could.

Bewildered, lonely and very depressed, I discovered I was pregnant, but there was no way that I would bring a child into that horrible environment. I was hungry, weak, and I felt my heart had been smashed into tiny pieces. I felt both hate and love for the man I left my home in England to be with.

My self-esteem and confidence, that had always been diminutive, were now almost zero. I totally hated this backward woman who could hardly read or write and who had no real brains or common sense. I also felt ugly, useless, and very unlucky. These were my thoughts at the time.

Though I felt this way about myself, I thought that whatever strength and confidence I had, I needed it for the children that I already had. I just couldn't bring another child into the world although, as an only child, it had been my dream to have an enormous family. I used to pray to God for eight children. I wanted a football team; I wanted seven boys and one girl.

While still living in the hotel, I made friends with a mixed-race lady who was a TV presenter. We became very close. Whenever I saw her on the television, I couldn't believe she was my friend. As I write my story, I am struggling to remember her face. I can see her big brown afro hair and the outline of her light brown face, but I can't see her eyes, nose or the shape of her lips.

This lovely lady lent me her ears, and I exhausted them with my unfortunate stories about what was going on in my life at the time. I told her I was pregnant, but I was too hungry, weak and depressed to have the child and I hardly saw my fiancé. She introduced me to her best friend, who was a diplomat. By this time, she had already briefed her beforehand about me and what I was going through. Therefore, by the time we met, both of them had devised a plan for how they were going to help me.

When we met, she gave me a book I kept for years, with all the quotes from the bible where Jesus says he loves us, and we are all special. I believed that God, being a man, hated me like the father of my children, and my own father too, who never spoke to me unless he was beating me. I had felt unloved all of my life until that day.

The diplomat told me a true story about a young lady she knew, whose life she believed was more tragic than mine, to make me feel I wasn't alone in my suffering.

The story starts with a young married woman with children, who is trying to live through a civil war in her country. During the war, her husband and children died in her arms and also her brother. She lost her parents in the war as well. To save her own life, she had to flee from her country and eventually she met the diplomat who was now narrating her story to me.

There was a lady cleaning her bathroom floor that was near to the living room door. The diplomat pointed to her and said, that is the lady whose story I just told you about.

I was quiet because I needed time to take it all in. I just kept looking at the woman who had endured so much sorrow and pain. It was more than just a story to me; it was a tragic account of the effects of war that I may never experience. When I looked at her, it all became so real; I knew I had not just watched a war film. Her story just flashed by me, and it was real, it wasn't in my mind. Looking at her as she peacefully cleaned the floor, I heard the gunshots, and I saw her child stretched out in her arms, lifeless, clothes dripping with blood. I saw her mouth open wide as she lamented her great loss.

For a moment, I stopped thinking about myself, as this true story filled my mind. But suddenly, I felt my pain, as hers faded away. I was looking at a woman who was now free; a desire that I yearned for at that moment. I felt so very trapped, and I was suffocating in my unfortunate circumstances, which made it hard to think about someone else's pain, even though it was obviously greater than my own. Her pain was far greater than mine. She had lost all of her family and I still had mine.

Most people would say it was my choice to go to Africa, but the way I interpret destiny is, if I could have seen the future, I would have chosen not to take that flight to Africa. That is why I allowed the Indian man into my house before I left England. I wanted him to show me the future and tell me not to go, but that didn't happen. Mother Nature blinds our eyes, so that we live in the present and move toward to future, no matter what may unfold for us.

I knew that with each movement as the woman wiped the floor dry with the cloth, she was crying out loud inside. As a mother, I knew this. I had travelled with my children to be with the man I loved, hoping to see my mother soon; I could not bear losing them or even imagine them dying in my arms. I knew her pain was much greater than mine, but all I felt was my pain as hers faded, as if I had just finished watching a film about war on the television.

We met at the diplomat's house to discuss what I wanted to do with the pregnancy. I was too depressed and weak to have a baby because I was hungry most of the time, and I didn't have any money to pay to have an abortion, so the diplomat and my celebrity friend offered to pay. I didn't tell the father of my children because I knew he didn't care about me; he didn't even care about his children, so I had the abortion without him knowing about it.

I can't remember anyone going with me to have it done. It wasn't a hospital. It was a small backstreet clinic, but it was a clean, professional environment, and there were no reasons for any concern. I was confident that I was going to be alright because I felt I had no choice. I was so hungry; my taste buds yearned for a Cornish pasty and fresh milk, but I would have got over this craving if I was loved and taken care of. I was so lost, confused and depressed. I didn't want to carry a child in a weak, afflicted body, only to be born into an environment where I had no money and there was barely enough for us to eat.

After the operation, the next day I was in a lot of pain and the day after that, too. Unfortunately, the abortion went terribly wrong, and I almost died. I really thought that I was going to die, but every time I thought of my daughter and my mother, I suddenly gained the strength to stay alive. My daughter's father died when she was three months old. Therefore, I knew that if anything happened to me, my boy's father and his family would take care of them, but I wasn't sure if they would have loved my daughter. As for my mother, she would have died with a broken heart not knowing if I was dead or alive; I was her only child.

After the abortion, they left most of the embryo inside me, so I was haemorrhaging. One day, my fiancé's cousin came to see us, and I told her what had happened. I asked her to look after my son while the other two stayed with his mother. He was very hyperactive, and I thought it would be too much responsibility for his grandmother. They must have told my fiancé, because we had not seen him for some time. When he came to the hotel, I remember there being no remorse and empathy in his body language. He drove me to the hospital with a friend to remove all that was left in me after the abortion. After the operation, I got a chest infection that lasted for months because of the stress, and the fact that my problems were far from over; if anything, they had just begun.

And so, my plight continued. I often took a taxi to my fiancé's workplace to ask him for money. The first time I went there after my first arrival in the country, his boss was very shocked and concerned. The first time we met, my baby boy was just over a year old, so I was looking a little stout and very healthy because I had not long stopped nursing him. Now, I was very thin, my face was gaunt, and the whites of my eyes were slightly yellow and since I am a woman that shows her emotion, sadness was written all over me, and wearing me down.

I told my fiancé's boss that we lived in a hotel and I had to walk nearly two miles with my children to his mother's house to eat. He gave us a loan for a deposit to rent a property that would be deducted from his wages each month. He cared so much for me and the children, he wanted us to live in the company house on the premisses, but the father of my children declined his offer. Eventually, the father of my children saw a house that was suitable to rent, but his pregnant girlfriend told the landlord that she knew him very well. She said he was a dishonest person and could not be trusted, so the landlord gave him back the deposit, which he wasted. I heard that he also paid for hospital expenses for his pregnant girlfriend. I was furious when I heard this, so I took some of the money to buy clothes for me and the children, and I gave some to his brother who was very sick.

It was on that day that we had a big, heated quarrel that led to me taking off my ring and throwing it at him. That was also the day on which I decided that, one day, I would tell my story, but I had to learn to read and write properly first; and I knew it would be a monumental challenge for me. I didn't know how I was going to do it or if I would ever leave Africa. It was also on that day, after sobbing like a child, that I got drunk and went to bed after smoking my fiancé's cigarettes.

Nevertheless, the aftermath of what had happened since I arrived in Africa had made me more mature in my thinking; for example, the way I looked at life and my destiny. The next morning, I felt different. I had always felt like a girl, but now, for the first time, I felt like a woman. I awoke realising that my six-year relationship had ended, there wasn't going to be a wedding and there was no way my mother could join us. I was now more spiritually aware. Also, I now had the ability to point the finger at myself and take some responsibility for what was happening to me, which I wouldn't have dreamt of doing before.

When I first met my fiancé, I wasn't happy. He always said that one day he would make me happy. I came to realise that no one could make me happy but myself. Only I could heal myself from the deep wounds that happened when I was a child, but I didn't know where to start. However, one thing was certain: I knew I could never be the person I was born to be while living in Africa, although I had always wanted to live there. I had to return home to England, but how was I going to do this? My tickets had expired, and I didn't have any money to return home.

My fiancé was more desperate for me to return home than I was. After everything that had happened, I was still holding on to my dream of living and raising my children in Africa, but he was looking for reasons to convince his family that I was useless. He was convinced that I was a very unlucky person, and it would be better for everyone if I went home. He saw me as an illiterate woman who couldn't do anything right. Strange how he didn't think like this before. One evening, I was sitting with my fiancé and his friend at a table in the hotel where we were living, when my feet touched something hard underneath it. I looked to see what it was, and I was so shocked to find it was the stone that I had thrown out of the window after he had thrown my engagement ring out of the window and left the room weeks ago. The window was right at the back of the hotel, whereas we were now sitting at the front, and although there were about twelve to fifteen tables in the restaurant, the stone still ended up under our table. So, the shock of seeing the stone was written all over my face. When he saw the expression on my face, he wanted to know what was wrong. Was this a coincidence, or did the stone appear miraculously under our table because I disobeyed the Indian man when he told me not to tell anyone that he had given it to me? We will never know, but I was going to disobey him again, because I was about to tell him how I got it. This was also a chance for me to talk to him and get his attention, for once.

He asked me what the matter was and sadly, I told him what had happened and where I had got the stone from. I told him that an Indian man came to the house and gave it to me for good luck. At first, he was very upset that I had done such an ungodly thing, but now he had the perfect excuse for me to go home. In the family meeting, he told them that the stone was bad luck, and I had bewitched our relationship, and that was why it all went wrong. "It is all your fault", he said with great conviction. I believed this for years, but not any more. He took the stone and said he would give it to someone who might know more about it. I remember once the car broke down, and he thought it was my fault because of the stone and sadly I believed him. I am laughing now as I share this with you.

Five months had gone by since we had arrived, but it seemed like five years. We were still living in the hotel, and the only time I saw him was when he had an argument with his girlfriends. Yes, girlfriends. Apparently, they always argued over me, because they wanted him to send me home, but he didn't have the money to do that. Whenever they had an argument, he would come back to the hotel furious and take it out on me, but I had no idea what was going on.

I discovered he had more than one girlfriend, when his sister introduced me to a lady from an English-speaking country in Africa so I would have someone to talk with. I told her about his cousin who I really loved because she was so kind to me and my children. I told her the cousin's name. She gasped for air after hearing her name. Apparently, the cousin wasn't really his cousin, she was his girlfriend, so he had two!

Like his pregnant girlfriend, I had kissed her, too, when I first arrived in his country, not knowing who she was; she even took me to a club once to cheer me up. She used to bring chips to the hotel because we were from England, and she thought that's what we liked to eat.

I remember him introducing her to me as his cousin, though he denied it later. He thought I had mistaken her for his cousin, but she was tall and lived in the house with us, whereas his girlfriend was short with a round face and sightly resembled my soul-friend.

She saved my life because she kept on coming to the hotel to see if my child's dad was there. So, when I was haemorrhaging after I had had the abortion, she was able to help me; but she was only looking for him. Apparently, she assumed that if he wasn't with me, he was with the other woman.

When my friend told me who she was, I felt humiliated. I felt betrayed because I really believed she was his cousin. I once told him that I loved her, and she was my favourite among his family because she was so kind to me and my children. Now, I was seething with revenge and couldn't wait to confront her. One thing about me, I never run away from any battle. When I eventually saw her, I sat next to her and looked her in the eyes, and told her I knew who she really was and one day she would pay for what she was doing to me and my children. I didn't take my eyes off her until she looked away, not in shame, but in victory because, in her mind, she knew he would marry *her* one day. That day, she must have told him what had happened because that evening, when he came back to the hotel, he burst into the room. He was very, very angry. His eyes were red, and you could see the anger and frustration in them. The hate he felt for me was as clear as clean water in a glass. I could never hate him; throughout all the turbulence in our relationship, I realised how much I loved him, but I was so disappointed that he had invited me to Africa only to make me cry. Perhaps he didn't realise he would feel that much hate towards me or else he wouldn't have allowed me to join him in his homeland.

That night, he slept at the hotel. His girlfriends were probably angry and frustrated with him. My friend from Cameroon told me they kept telling him to send me home.

Though I didn't hate him, I wanted some kind of revenge. I wanted him to feel as trapped and as confused as I did, but how was I going to let him know how I was feeling?

The only thing I could do was this: as soon as he was fast asleep, I dressed him in my tight nightdress and when he woke up in the morning, he almost broke his neck as he tried to walk to the bathroom before realising what he was wearing. I couldn't stop laughing as I covered my head with the sheet and made a little hole to watch him stagger across the room. He was so angry. He never said a word to me, and I didn't ask why.

21 August 1989

It was my birthday and I had lost all hope of being happy in Africa, and I didn't know if I would ever return to England. I had no money. The children and I barely had anything to eat. Being illiterate, with basic communication skills, there was no way of making a living to save the money to return to England. It was my birthday, and he made an effort to make me happy, at least for one day. A few of his friends came to the hotel and we ate and drank wine to celebrate. I was drinking Nigerian Guinness. I tried to relax, but it was difficult. I knew the next day was going to be like every other day. But it was the first time I had had wine since I gave birth to my son, and it was also the first time I had seen my fiancé relaxed with me since we had arrived. So, I really made an effort to pretend that all was well.

That night, he stayed at the hotel and drove us to his mother's house in the morning before going to work. His mother's place was a place to socialise with the rest of the family and sometimes visitors came. The neighbours were very close; they were like family. My children could play with their cousins, and I could go for a very long walk. I often told his mother in her language that "I am going out, I'll be back".

One day, I walked into an empty church, knelt down and began praying earnestly from the very depths of my desperate lonely soul as I cried out to God when suddenly I felt a gentle hand touch my shoulder. It surprised me because I was the only one there, and I heard no footsteps prior to the strange touch. Though the tears blurred my eyes, when I looked up, I saw a tall, dark, slender man looking down at me with tenderness in his eyes. He shook his head slightly as he tilted it to one side in wonder. I said "hello". It surprised me that he said hello back in an American accent. "Where are you from?", he asked, as he gently helped me up from my knees. That was the beginning of a platonic friendship that lasted for a very long time. From that day on, he helped me to carry my troubles by lending me his shoulder and his ears. The church was also a school, so he was more than happy for my son to attend classes free of charge.

The time came when we had to leave the hotel to live permanently with my children's grandmother. The first night I slept there, I woke up to find cockroaches and insects crawling all over my children, even in their eyes and their noses, just like what had happened to me in my dream nearly six years ago. At the time, I knew this feeling was connected to my fiancé. I hadn't been able to discern these creatures so I thought they were foreign, but they were bugs that you can find in any country. Now, the bad feeling I had carried for so long had gone when the dream came true. I began to pray even more for God to help me to return home to England than ever before.

Was it ordained before my birth that I should meet this man, have his children, travel to Africa only to be rejected and to cry a pool of tears and return home in despair?

When we moved in with (by now) my ex-fiancé's mother, he was never there. He didn't sleep there, not even for one night. He only came when he was summoned by the family either for the family meeting or if there was a problem. Sometimes, his brother and I used to argue, then suddenly he would turn up. But he never had anything to say to me, other than "you love each other", as in brother and sister love. They would have had to go to his workplace to tell him we were arguing, because they didn't have mobiles and there was no phone in the house. Other than that, he came every month to a family meeting hosted by his uncle, whom I call "papa". At the end of the meeting, the solution was that we would live at his uncle's house because they all thought our main problem was that we didn't have a place of our own. But we never went there to live. Every family problem would be addressed with a solution except for ours. Our problem was discussed last, often in the early hours of the morning. Apart from living with his "papa", the other alternative was that I would return home to England, but because there was no money to buy our tickets that was out of the question.

The only thing I could do was to continue praying. I prayed in my heart throughout the day. When I awoke in the morning, I didn't wait to get off the bed to kneel down to pray; I prayed as soon as I opened my eyes, I prayed to God. I didn't know what else to do. I had not money and power.

One day, I took a taxi to his office to ask him for money. By now, I was used to sharing my taxi with other people. The first time I took a taxi, I was furious when the taxi driver picked up other people. I told them all to get out of the car. When I arrived at my destination, my fiancé had to pay for all the people that I had told to get out, so I learnt from that mistake. This was the only culture shock that I had to get over quickly because, unaware, I was going to meet a passenger who would help destiny prevail in my life because I was praying and sending out the right signals in the Universe to work on my behalf. If I had met this passenger in the early days, I would have told him to get out of the car.

One day, I shared a taxi with an African American. By now, I was used to sharing the taxi. As soon as I realised he spoke English, I began telling him my story in the car. I couldn't stop talking and I still can't stop talking; I am hoping that after the publication of this book, I will finally put my past to rest in perfect peace. He told me I had touched his heart with my story and from that moment on we became friends. I can't remember if I ever got to my destination because I ended up at his house, eating dinner his wife had cooked.

However, this friendship was short-lived because his wife thought I wanted a relationship with him, which was far, far away from my mind.

The African American was a part of my destiny that would help me do something about my situation, instead of just praying. He told me that if he got stranded in Africa, the American Embassy would help him return home even if he had no money, so he advised me to go to the British Embassy. Unfortunately, when I went there, they told me they couldn't help because I wasn't British, although I was born in England. They told me that Australians were more British than I was. It was like someone had put a hot dagger in my heart and it stopped for a second because I was so shocked and so very confused. I had never heard this before. I couldn't believe what I was hearing. I was more lost and confused than when I entered the building; I was very embarrassed too. I was born in a racist country that did not recognise me as British; although I used to say that the Queen of England would never take me as her own, nevertheless, I still couldn't believe what they were saying to me. I really felt like throwing away my passport.

They didn't allow me to go away empty-handed. They told me the only thing they could do for me was to forward a letter to my mother on my behalf, and they also gave me a list of English-speaking churches I could attend in order to socialise with people from English-speaking countries.

When I went back to his mother's house, I wrote a letter to my mother. I recall writing the letter with a sorrowful heart and being more determined this time than before when I quit and placed the pen down on the bed, and sat on the floor for hours weeping because I couldn't find the words to express myself It was just one paragraph with two simple sentences that I didn't know that they were called so at the time: "Mum, things are not working out for me and the children. Please help us to come home". The first time I tried to write to my mother, I couldn't because I wanted to tell her everything that was happening to us and I just didn't know the words to express all of that.

My body wanted to return home because it was heavily burdened with the labour of grief and pain, but my heart wanted to stay because it was my dream to live in Africa with my children's father. I wanted my children to grow up as Africans, but this dream never came true. His uncle said to me that his girlfriends had put voodoo on him, and when it wears off, his heart would be mine again. But although I wanted that so much, I knew it was better for me to go home. If he was truly mine, I couldn't have lost him. This was what I thought at the time, and I was really missing my mother and I wanted to drink fresh milk, not powered milk that made sick.

I took the embassy's advice and went to an American church where I met English-speaking people from all ethnic backgrounds. A few of them were happily married to the natives of the country and they thought I was very unlucky! I remember a lady saying, "You are very unlucky". But she didn't tell me anything I didn't already know. I have always thought I was unlucky and was responsible for all the bad luck in my life.

I remember having dinner with an African American family and a white English woman who I met at the church. Even the minister of the church invited me and my children to his home. So, looking back, I wasn't that unlucky because people wanted to help me. The minister lived in a very big house and the garden was huge, with all types of fruit trees my two eldest children tried to pick. He listened to me and counselled me; if my mother couldn't raise the money for us to return, the church would help. They had it all planned. The church minister also wrote to my mother on my behalf and told her everything that was happening to me. He told her the church was going to help me return home, so she shouldn't worry. For the first and last time in my life, I had many people around me supporting me. I wasn't lonely in Africa; I was just lonesome for the man I went there to marry.

December 1989

I went to the Embassy to see if my mother had written back to me, only to discover our tickets had arrived and were at the travel agency. Though I felt disappointed that our time in Africa didn't work out, I was exceedingly happy and so very grateful to God that we were going home. I was also grateful to the African American who had advised me to go to the Embassy. Despite the Embassy being racist and telling me I wasn't British, at least they sent my letter to my mother and, if it wasn't for the Embassy, I would not have met the church minister who also wrote to my mother.

When I returned to the family house, I didn't tell the family for nearly a week that I had received the tickets from my mother to return to England. In those days, it was a common belief that African men would try to take children away from their mothers, if a relationship ended, especially if the mother was from any of the western countries. There were many accounts of both black and white mothers stranded in Africa and forced to leave without their children; a few either had a nervous breakdown or died, and I was afraid he wouldn't allow my children to go home with me. Looking back now, I wish that I had been strong enough to leave my boys. I honestly believe they would have been better off with their family. Eventually, they would have had a lot of brothers and sisters to play with and would have grown up to understand family life and values, whereas I brought them up in isolation without any family around, except from my mother. It takes a village to raise a child; you cannot do it alone.

After we left the hotel to live with my ex-fiancé's mother, I often went for long walks. Therefore, my plan was that I would continue to go for my daily walks, but each time I would take some of our clothes to my friend's house. The day would come when I would have taken all my clothes, then I would leave the house with my children and never return. I now know that if I had accomplished this plan, it would have been one of the biggest mistakes I could have made, because, through the years, I have become very close to his family – both those who live in Africa and also those in the western world.

One day, I was talking to my children's dad's two brothers and their wives, and they conveyed to me how saddened there were by my situation. I knew in my heart that they were genuine, and it was then that I told them our tickets had arrived, and we were going home that very weekend. They couldn't have been more shocked when I told them I would travel that very week. They asked me where I got the money from? I told them my mother had raised it after I wrote to her. They wanted to know how I managed to post the letter to my mother as there were no post boxes to post letters and the post office was very far away, so it would have been too expensive to take a taxi there. But nothing could stop me from trying to help myself out of a situation I had got myself into, just because I couldn't see into the future. Therefore, I used my unfortunate situation to my advantage. Sometimes, taxi drivers would take me wherever I wanted to go, when I told them my story, and by then I could also speak their language a little.

The family was so relieved for me. From their body language and what they said, I saw genuine benevolence towards me. So, when they advised me to go home and find a husband to take care of me and the children, I knew they said it from their hearts. The family further confirmed how much they cared for both me and the children when they declared they were mine. "They are your children, not our brother's", thy shamefully admitted with regret on his behalf. One of his brothers' wives said he didn't deserve them because he was irresponsible.

The next day, they summoned papa to the house for a family meeting and he was told the good news everyone was waiting for. Word also reached the ladies in the market, although it confused me as to how they got to know. The news also reached my children's dad. When he came to the house and realised that the new about us going home was true, he didn't know how to react. I could see he was filled with different emotions. He was shocked, ashamed, sad, happy and relieved. And believe me, I felt all that too, and more. I was going home a single mother. I was afraid of bringing up my three children without a father and a family. I was never close to my mother's family and I didn't know my father's family.

Friday, 8 December 1989

Finally, the day came when the children and I were leaving. All the family was there, even papa, the uncle who used to facilitate the family meetings each month because we had a meeting the night before. We were going to leave very early in the morning, and all I can say is, I felt loved. They showered the children with much love, care and attention. Do you see now if I didn't tell them that I was leaving, it would have been a terrible mistake.

Anyway, after the children had eaten their last evening meal on African soil, their aunties bathed them and put them to bed. The evening was very relaxing. Our time in Africa was coming to an end. Throughout the night until early hours in the morning, I went to bed while the father of my children and the family continued talking. The family advised me to go home and find a husband, but I knew it would not be that easy. My conviction was right, because as I write all this down, I am not married, although I know it is never too late.

In the morning, my ex-fiancé's sister and his sister-in-law bathed and fed the children again and gave them tea and bread. When it was time for us to leave, everyone wanted to come to the airport with us, but it was not possible; there weren't enough cars to take everyone. My ex-fiancé's mother cried and held onto her grandchildren, especially the baby. She pulled him out of my arms because maybe subconsciously she knew she would never see him again – and she never did. I took him back as they were rushing us to leave. We hugged and kissed those we were leaving behind and sadly said our goodbyes.

Arriving at the airport, my ex-fiancé's took his children into his arms and held on to them tightly. Not knowing the future, I had no idea this would be the last time he would hold his children in his arms and tell them he loved them. He told us he would join us in England, but that day never came. I wrapped my arms around him and didn't want to let go. At that moment I knew how much I had loved him. My love for him was undying. I loved him then, and I still do, as I narrate my story to you. And it is not because I don't love myself because I have grown to first like, and then love, myself. You can't help who you love, but that doesn't mean you are meant to stay together.

As I held on to him, I advised him to take good care of himself. I promised to pray for him, to pray that he would meet a wonderful woman to love and take care of him, for the sake of his children, so we would meet again.

When I boarded the plane, I left a piece of me in Africa. I was both happy and very sad that I was leaving the Motherland. As the plane opened it's wing and took off and flew up into the great blue, warm African sky, I remembered how I used to walk on its golden hot soil to mama's place.

Suddenly, my baby began crying and wriggling his body. I took him to the toilet and was utterly shocked when I saw long white roundworms coming out of his bottom. I knew then that I was doing the right thing in leaving Africa.

Ebery spwoil mek a style

If something goes wrong do not fret, use this mishap to your advantage to create something new.

The use of serendipity with creativity is wonderful advice.

Everal McKenzie

Chapter Three

My Return to the Motherland (30 Years Later)

Sunday, 8 December 2019

Thirty years later (to the very date), once again, I was in the Motherland, but this time not to start a new life, but sadly to celebrate the life and death of the father of my children. I arrived in Africa without my children at 11:55 p.m. and by 12:30 a.m. when they had completed all the formalities, I began walking towards the glass doors that would lead me out of the airport. As they opened, I felt the cool, warm air go right through me; it made me feel so relaxed. My fiancés niece was the first person I saw, with her arms spread open as wide as she could to welcome me.

"Tatie" (aunty) she yelled out in French, with a joyous, wide smile across her face, as the doors opened, and I hastened to towards her opened arms. We recognised each other because we were friends on Facebook. We had to wait for about twenty minutes for her cousin. The last time I had seen him was in Europe when he was a little boy; now he was a grown man with seven children. He couldn't wait to hug and kiss me and take selfies of us together; he was so happy to see me, and I was very happy to see him. The smiles and greetings lasted for only a short while because we were now going to drive to where my fiancé's body rested before the funeral. In my parents' home town they call this part of the burial Nine-Night, or the Dead Yard.

As I approached the hall where his body lied for all to see and pay their respects, I was welcomed with beautiful, colourful African traditional dancing, while some people were sleeping on the floor. The Nine-Night had started the night before and by the time I got there it was in the early hours of the third day, so there was no time to sleep. In the early afternoon, we went to his house to bathe and ordain ourselves, especially for his funeral.

Every so often the mourners walked around the coffin, lamenting. It was a bitter-sweet moment to see both love and sincere sorrow combined when celebrating the life of a man who was too young to die. But we know that the Angel of Death does not discriminate when deciding who to take next. His niece in America told me they were expecting others to die in the family, but not him. He left behind his elder siblings and even his old aunties and Papa (uncle), who was the primary host of family meetings, since his father had died in the early 1970s. But, most tragically, he also left behind twelve children and stepchildren.

The woman to whom my he had introduced me thirty years ago as his cousin, but really she was his girlfriend, lovingly took my hand and walked with me around the coffin. Though she had married him when I left Africa and had two boys by him, I welcomed this gesture because one of the reasons I was desperate to go to the funeral was to forgive all and let go, not just for me, but also for my children, and my children's children. I also wanted to close the chapter on that part of my life, because I kept holding on to it tightly.

After the first time she held my hand and led me around the coffin, when we returned to our seats, I felt her energy pulling me. I turned to face her, and at that moment our eyes clashed. I had done her no wrong, so I felt no guilt when I gazed deep into her eyes the way I did thirty years ago. The muscles in my face were as still as a cloudless sky, but I felt no hate towards her, only anger, but not an anger that desired destruction. I knew in my heart that I would continue this fixation until she looked away in pure shame and regret, as she did thirty years ago. And as it should be, she then closed her eyes and opened them again as she looked away, and down onto the floor, and then at the coffin. Only then did I stop looking at her, as we both began to look at the man we both loved. At that point, the daughter of his other girlfriend, who was pregnant when I was in Africa, came and sat on the floor between my legs, and I felt pure love for her. She looked just like her father and my eldest son.

After I had dealt with that part of my past, I got up and stood beside my fiancé's coffin and began talking to him. I was crying inside, but my eyes were as dry as a desert, and I felt like a solid stone. I was the same at my mother's funeral. It wasn't until after I had buried my mother that I began to cry, which I continued to do for years. Now and then, I still shed a tear for her, and I always will.

As I leaned over the coffin and placed my hand on the glass covering, I thanked him for the children and for inviting me to Africa. I asked him to bless the children, if he could. I told him that I understood that he fell out of love with me, but he could have tried harder to make my stay in Africa as pleasant as possible until I returned home. I told him that I forgave him, and that I have learnt, over the years, to take some responsibility for all that happened back then. I also told him to say hello to my mother.

Immediately, after I had mentioned my mother, for the first time in my life, I suddenly had a feeling of déjà vu that all this had happened before and at exactly the same time. I told him this in my mind. According to scientific research, people often experience déjà vu in times of high pressure and stress. I must have been more stressed then I thought. I was very stressed that my children would never see their father again. But this doesn't explain what happened after that thought came to me. While I was experiencing déjà vu, I had a strong feeling that something bad was going to happen. I asked my ex-fiancé what was going to happen to me. That same day, my bag was stolen along with my passport and my phone and other important documents. It was a living nightmare! But I had to put it out of my mind in order to take part in the funeral procession later that day. It wasn't until after his body was laid to rest that I began to ask myself how I was going to return home.

All those years ago, the British Embassy told me in Africa that, even though I was born in England, Australians were more British than I was, and they couldn't help me. Destiny prevailed and, thirty years later, I returned to the Embassy wiser and more confident to demand my rights as a (British West Indian) for help to return to England, although I wasn't going to ask them for financial help to return home. Surprisingly, all the staff were black and very welcoming, professional and supportive.

They gave my nephew a list of instructions to carry out in order for them to issue me with a temporary passport. The terrifying truth is, if I hadn't emailed a copy of my passport to my nephew, I would have been stranded in Africa!

We first had to go to the police station to get a written and stamped report about what had happened, and what was in my bag, but when I arrived there, I was more upset with the condition of the police station than I was about the fact that someone stolen my passport. The shed in my garden in England was a palace compared to the police station and I was very, very angry with the African government in allowing its citizens, whose job it is to protect the people and maintain law and order, to work in such appalling conditions.

It was an old, rundown shed, just big enough for the interviewee and interviewer. They didn't have a computer, only an old mobile phone. The rest of the police officers were stationed outside, sitting on chairs on the muddy ground. I couldn't help thinking about the police officer's salary and where he lived. The actions of the police officer reflected my concerns about his domestic life because he was trying to overcharge us. In my opinion, it wasn't corruption; it was survival! Therefore, my concerns were right about his financial circumstances. If I were rich, there is no way I would have left those police officers in those conditions.

Apparently, since the last time I was there, the country's socio-economics had declined. I was furious and extremely disturbed to see how severe the poverty was in the country; I decided that as soon as I returned home, I would write a letter to the President to urge him to do something about it.

When I finally arrived home, I wrote to all the African leaders; pleading with them to unite, protect the people and Africa's natural resources for the benefit of the people. However, due to the COVID-19 pandemic, I couldn't post the letter, so I published it on Amazon instead and is part two of this book I am hoping to post the letter to all African leaders in 2023, when I publish this story.

In 2019, thirty years after I had left Africa, I couldn't even write a simple compound descriptive letter to my mother to tell her all that I was going through in that country; but now I was considering writing to the heads of state. I didn't even know the words, simple, compound and descriptive.

What I forgot to tell you earlier is that after I left the British Embassy in 1989 where they refused to help me return to England, I went to look for a job. I must have realised that it was the only way I was going to raise the money to return home. I found a British oil firm that was prepared to give me work and pay me $100 per month to do secretarial work. But I was only fooling myself because although I could do copy typing, I couldn't read or write properly, so the plan was that I would go home and write a basic letter to my mother to ask her to help me.

The question is, what happened to me? Why, at thirty years old, was I unemployable and struggling to write a letter to my mother, although I was born and raised in England, where education is free and compulsory? The next chapter will answer this question.

Subnormal Education

The teacher sat with us at the dinner table

to teach us how to eat with a knife, fork and spoon.

We had to sit up straight, elbows off the table

and slowly scrape a tiny portion of each food onto the back of the fork with the knife,

put it slowly into our mouths with our backs still straight

and eat with dignity.

We were not allowed to speak with food in our mouths.

So, when I left school, I could eat like the Queen of England,

but I couldn't read and write or talk like her.

Chapter Four

It Takes a Whole Village to Raise a Child: (My English Racist Teachers)

It is 1964 and I am about to be taken care of by society because it takes a group to raise a young one. I was about to start school to meet the teachers who would help my parents to prepare me for a prosperous future, and what better place to be educated than England; a country West Indians called the mother country, sometimes referred to as the parent country. My parents had nothing to worry about. It was like leaving me in the care of a grandparent.

As my mother and I walked into my classroom with the teacher, all the children turned and stared at me – not my mum, just me – as we walked to the front of the classroom. When I realised my mother was going to leave me there, I panicked and clung tightly onto her dress. I felt like a plank of wood as I froze with fear, with my heart throbbing, yet I would often wander away from home, alone, with no fear, but fear was always a part of me.

Eventually, as time went on, I couldn't wait to go to school. I realised it was a better place to be than at home because my teachers were all nice and I enjoyed playtimes inside as well as outdoors activities, but only when the weather was warm.

At Christmas, unlike at home, you could sense it was Christmas, and it was my favourite season of the year. I enjoyed Christmas dinners, parties, getting presents, designing Christmas trimmings and putting them up because I was very creative. At home, we never had a Christmas tree or decorations, but mum brought me presents. I always got a white doll for Christmas and sweets. Dad's friends came over, as usual, and it was a merry time in some ways; but only for the adults. Most of the time, I was the only child among the adults, but I had a great imagination.For my first Christmas play at school, they chose me to play Angel Gabriel. I know it was the first one because, for my second Christmas, I was placed in the ESN school. I was very nervous because I thought I would stutter, but knowing that my mother was in the audience made me feel relaxed. I played the part splendidly and I didn't stammer. I remember thinking that I wanted to play Angel Gabriel again, but it never happened.

While Christmas was my favourite time of the year, story time was my favourite time of the day. I was most relaxed at this time because I didn't have to learn anything. All I had to do was listen. Keeping absolutely still was not a problem for me. I would fully immerse myself in the story and pretend to be the main hero, acting out their part in my mind. I couldn't just sit there and listen without being a part of the story. I would block out everything around me and completely immerse myself in it. I did the same when watching a film.

When the teachers closed the book, and the story was over, I couldn't wait to get my hands on the book. But whenever I opened it, it was just black lines on white paper moving about, like the lines on a train track. As time went on, I noticed that other children were beginning to read a little, but the book never worked for me, and it still doesn't. I call myself a research reader, like students. I mostly skim and scan as I look for information as a writer. I have never read a book from beginning to end for pleasure.

IT TAKES A WHOLE VILLAGE TO RAISE A CHILD: (MY ENGLISH RACIST TEACHERS)

One day, the school invited my mother for a meeting with the head teacher. After the meeting, I was called into the room and told to sit down. The head teacher gave me some instructions. She said, "get up, open the door, go downstairs; all the way to the bottom, then come back up the stairs again".

I did exactly what she told me to do. Based on my performance, she told my mother that I was backward, and I had to go to a special school. This was what my mother told my father at home. The teacher gave me something to carry, so I think that's where I went wrong, because I came back with something in my hand, but I can't remember what it was. My mother didn't understand. I was at the age when I should be reading, so she thought a special school would help. She didn't know that I would receive a subnormal education. She didn't realise that I was an intelligent child, who needed a lot of support while remaining in a mainstream school, whereas my teachers were fully aware of my capabilities and my needs, because they were teachers, but they chose to ignore my needs because they didn't want to give me the extra support I needed due to their racist convictions.

It wasn't until I was thirty-eight years old that I discovered I was dyslexic, when I did a psychological assessment. I was doing an Access course in Modern Music, and my teachers advised me to get tested for dyslexia. They recognised dyslexic traits that my teachers in my infant school should have been aware of, although dyslexia wasn't as well-recognised as it is today.

The earliest reference to dyslexia was in the late Victorian period. The doctors of that period first identified the condition as "word blindness" in enabled children showing reading difficulties.

The British Dyslexia Association was formed in 1972. Therefore, this is evidence that, in the '60s, teachers would have had some basic knowledge about dyslexia due to discourse around the subject before forming the association. They would have recognised the early signs of dyslexia; in my case, for example, the way I absorbed and retrieved information and the time it took me to do so.

Moreover, it was obvious that I couldn't carry out instructions, which is a sign of dyslexia caused by short-term working memory, but the head teacher ignored this too when I was told to go downstairs and come back up and I forgot the other instructions. I just needed a lot more time and more support in the classroom. I noticed that extra support was given to a few English children who sat together, and the teacher would repeat to them what they had said to the rest of us. These were the children who stayed behind in class while we went out to play; that was exactly the support which I needed, but the teachers preferred to send me off into an environment that would continue to ignore my learning needs.

When my mother told me I was going to leave my school, I started crying. I was telling my mother that I didn't want to leave the school, when I felt a sudden blow to my back. At first, I didn't know what it was, but within seconds I realised that my father had hit me with considerable force; I felt as though my eardrums had exploded, so loud was the blow to my back. I knew exactly what my dad wanted me to do. He wanted me to be quiet, and to appreciate that I was going to a special school. So I tried to force myself to stop crying, although the tears were falling down my cheeks and I was trying to catch my breath, which made me sound as though I was out of breath and had hiccups at the same time. It petrified me that if I uttered one more sound, I would get a full-blown beating. I was too young to understand the implication of going to a special school and I was upset that I was leaving my friend behind.

Slowly, slowly, I calmed myself down and dried my tears, as I suppressed my feelings because they didn't count because I was just a child. I walked sadly across the room and sat on the chair and started watching television. I was a big soul in a tiny body, looking up at these two giants who didn't have a clue about raising a child. Either my mother was afraid to stop my father from hitting me or she felt it was not her place as a woman to tell a man – her husband – what to do. I guess they were products of their time.

Being colonial migrants, they trusted the British education system created by the very people who perceived them as sub-humans and called them monkeys; monkeys who worked for them as slaves for hundreds of years; monkeys who fought their wars and afterwards, from 1948 onwards, they left their homelands to help them rebuild their economy by doing the jobs the natives refused to do. Therefore, I was going to a school in England and that was all that mattered to them, especially my dad.

To be fair to my mother, if she stood up to my father, she probably would have received a big blow to her head by his hands or something hard. Perhaps it was the time she lived in because I wouldn't have stayed with a man like that.

In the first school, I used to recite my tables in front of the class, but I can't remember doing this when I went to the ESN school and, sadly, I still do not know my times tables. Writing this has taken me back to when I was in my twenties as a young mother, a time when I couldn't read to my children or help them with their times tables.

In the mainstream school, the teachers were always talking to us and teaching us something, but in the ESN school, when the teacher wasn't reading to us, sometimes we played with a toy in the corner of the room or read a book; in my case, I would read the pictures. I remember drawing a lot and also using tracing paper to draw and write letters. When I went to the ESN junior school, I continued using tracing paper to write numbers and letters until I left school. I remember I was tracing letters when I told my teacher I wanted to be put in care because I was very unhappy at home. I was thirteen years old.

There was one activity we used to do that was racist. The teachers used to draw profiles of our faces and compare them to other children whose features were more European. I was told I had nice features because of my straight nose, which was the first positive thing any teacher had told me, but I didn't know then that this was racist. And in any case, how would this activity and comment help me in my life?

Notably disturbing, there was no proper arrangement or curriculum because, if there had been, they wouldn't have allowed me to stay in the classroom and make a puppet show to amuse the children when they came in. The reality is, the children would only come in to spend their time drawing or playing with toys. My thoughts were occupied and full of stories, and I just wanted to entertain.

While I was entertaining the children, my teachers were intelligent enough to see that here was a child who had the skills to be either an actress or a writer, or perhaps both. Even if they wanted to help

IT TAKES A WHOLE VILLAGE TO RAISE A CHILD: (MY ENGLISH RACIST TEACHERS)

me, they couldn't, because they had to abide by the rules of the British Education System to suppress me, so I would become nothing important in society.

Instead of teaching us to read and write, we were taught how to wash ourselves. I was later asked to wash the children who had severe learning difficulties. In addition to this, the teacher sat with us at the dinner table to teach us how to eat with a knife, fork and spoon. We had to sit up straight, elbows off the table and slowly scrape a tiny portion of each food onto the back of the fork with the knife, put it slowly into our mouths with our backs still straight and eat with dignity. We were not allowed to speak with food in our mouths. So, when I left school, I could eat like the Queen of England, but I couldn't read and write or talk like her.

Eventually, when I went to a mainstream school, I used to call my former school a 'free school' because I realised that they did not teach me anything. At the mainstream school, we couldn't do as we pleased. We went to different lessons, in different classes, whereas in the ESN school, you stayed in the same class. It was a busy environment which I did not like. There was a considerable amount of teaching. I often felt my mind being swamped with information and I would just unplug because I wasn't used to it. Being made educationally subnormal resulted in me having a lazy attitude back then, throughout my life and in all areas of my life.

In the ESN school, the teachers had a lot of time to waste, so they often took us for tea and biscuits at someone's house; I don't know who this person was. While the teacher drank tea, we had orange juice and one biscuit because the teacher said we could only have one. We went on holidays if we were good, too. I was always on my best behaviour, so I never missed a trip to the countryside, where we stayed for a week, or the seaside for a day. They also told us that if we were good, we would go to a good school. I didn't know what a good school was, but I wanted to go, I didn't even know I was in a bad school. However, I was told that they wouldn't choose me to go to a good school because they caught me kissing a boy when we were playing out.

My teachers should have told my parents about the areas where I could excel but, growing up in the '60s, who was going to encourage a black child to amount to greatness? My father wouldn't allow my mother to do anything about it anyway, although he used to call me to dance for his friends, who would pay me one pound because I was so good. At the very least he should have sent me to dance classes. I guess he was too busy adjusting to English culture and working hard to keep a roof over our heads, which was more important to him than his child's future. Our neighbour across the road used to send her granddaughter to dancing lessons.

As children, we paid the price for our parents' dreams to live and better their lives in England. The war also affected the Caribbean, so this meant there were few jobs and opportunities back home. However, although the war also affected England, the belief was that its streets were paved with gold, and they wanted some of that gold; however, they paid an enormous price for it because the next generation grew up confused and frustrated. They had to fight for equality, demanding their rights as Black British.

In truth, West Indians were not invited to England to improve their lives. They were invited to improve the lives of the British people by helping to rebuild the economy after the Second World War. The agenda was to give West Indians employment doing all the menial jobs, if they could get a place to live, because quite often this proved to be very difficult because of the colour of their skin; white landlords [often] refused to rent to them. The kind of jobs that were easily available to them were hospital positions, factory jobs, bus drivers, dustbin men and cleaners. Thereafter, the plan was to make sure that their children did the same jobs when they grew up, and since such children were perceived as inferior to white children, why not dump them in ESN schools, so they will grow up to become factory workers and street cleaners like their parents?

There was talk in the black community about the British education system failing their children. This could have been the reason why my mother contacted a black social worker, or perhaps the social worker contacted my mother. Anyway, the social worker invited us to her office where she gave me a professional educational psychological assessment. It was almost identical to the dyslexia assessment I had in my late thirties when I studied for an Access course in Modern Music. The outcome of that assessment was that I was an intelligent child, and she promised my mother that she would do her utmost to get me out of the ESN school. She kept her promise and I was sent me to a Girls High School, but it was too late.

At the Girls High School, they placed me in the bottom class, where most of the children were black and the white children were rebellious. And, for the first time, they introduced me to geography and history, and other subjects that had never been mentioned in the

ESN school. I realised that I liked history and geography, perhaps because of the images these subjects evoked in my mind. Both these subjects are visual, so I noticed that I could understand lectures better, but it was too late because, at thirteen years old, when I had to write about these subjects, I couldn't. After spending my crucial years in a special school, now I was expected to write about history and do biology; it was impossible and often I put my head on the desk and went to sleep. My brain felt as though it was getting overloaded with information – I just didn't have the patience to deal with learning, and so I often played truant from school.

At sixteen years old, when I left school, I still could hardly read or write, and didn't know what job I was going to do. I don't even think I thought about it much, and my mother never spoke about it either or ever asked me what I wanted to do as a career. I wanted to be an actor, but I had a profound stutter and no confidence or self-esteem, although I wouldn't have had any problems learning my lines as an actor as long as someone read them to me. Thereafter, I would have memorise my lines and rewrite them over and over again. When I was a child, I learnt to read a few verses in the Bible this way, when my mother read to me, and I memorised and repeated them, despite not being able to read other parts of the Bible. THANK YOU, MOTHER! If only you had stayed dedicated and communicated with me daily, my reading would have advanced and my vocabulary would have grown.

Though I didn't think that I was beautiful, I still wanted to be a model, like most girls but that would have been impossible I thought, the best thing for me to do was to meet a man with brains, get married and be a housewife and have eight children; seven boys and one girl.

The problem with this backup plan is that if you don't love yourself, how can you meet someone who will love you unconditionally? If you can't read or write properly, and you have very little vocabulary, how are you going to help your children with their homework and have a meaningful conversation with your partner or even with your children? For all these reasons, sometimes I was quiet. Though I had plenty to say, I never had the words to express myself because I was overloaded with images and information in my mind but no words to convey my thoughts. When I tried to speak, and I had the words to articulate what I desired to say, I frequently got panic attacks because I thought no one would be intrigued. I talked myself into believing that I would stammer and that people would laugh, anyway, so I was always quiet and as I grew older, I become more and more a loner.

Nevertheless, I became obsessed with getting married and having my family. I really thought having children would fill the deep hole in my life and heal that overwhelming feeling of loneliness which had haunted me for as long as I could remember, but they never did because children are not meant to fill the lives of lonely people. The desire to have a family was a mean and a selfish thought because I had nothing to offer my children or a partner, but I didn't know any better.

When I was nearly twenty years old, I left home and went to live in another city, where I worked in a few factories. I worked as a packer, but I was never fast enough; and even if I was good at it, packing wasn't what I wanted to do for the rest of my life; I was too ambitious. The jobs that I was educated to do, like cleaning, made me so very depressed.

I also worked in a restaurant, but I kept on making mistakes. A white girl actually asked me "where is the rhythm in you?", and that was just when making the tea. Then a black guy locked me in the fridge, I guess because he thought I was useless – I was so forgetful. They didn't know my story, and neither did I. Lack of confidence and self-esteem made up my body language. It didn't help that I had a stutter, was very slow in doing things and couldn't read and write properly. For the aforementioned reasons, when I told my manager at the restaurant that I was leaving, he actually sad that he was happy. If I had one percent confidence, it was now zero.

A school's education is not just about learning to read and write and studying subjects. Children go to school to learn how to learn, play and social skills, not only with other children, but with the teachers too who are responsible for helping to develop the child's talents, confidence and self-esteem even if their parents don't have the ability do so. In my opinion, this is the first stage of a child's development. It wasn't because I was a slow learner why I lacked these skills; I lacked them because both the Education and my parents failed me.

When children develop the necessary social learning skills, then it is time to teach them subjects to further support their development and their talents to shine through as they grow older. During the course of learning, they learn about time management, setting priorities and goals and how to structure their lives and face the challenges in life.

Unlike the schools I went to from six to thirteen years old, in a mainstream school, children are given homework to complete before certain deadlines. They learn to solve problems, do research and think

IT TAKES A WHOLE VILLAGE TO RAISE A CHILD: (MY ENGLISH RACIST TEACHERS)

and reason analytically. At school, children learn to develop networking and social skills. I did not learn these skills until I went to university at forty-one years of age. A lecturer at university once told me he couldn't fathom why I wrote the way I did, although I was dyslexic because other students who were dyslexic didn't write like me. At that moment, I didn't comprehend what he meant by that because I didn't realise that I was made educationally subnormal.

My social inadequacy became more apparent when I went to a mainstream school, when I had to adjust to structure, active listening, learning and communicating and doing activities in groups. Although I was in the lowest class, it was still a learning environment. I was so frustrated! I used to argue with my teachers and the children in the class, if they dared to make me feel inferior. I felt inferior, although I didn't know the word for that feeling at the time. I just didn't feel good enough; I felt stupid! I must have felt like a pet fish in a glass bowl that suddenly finds itself in the deep ocean. As I wrote previously, I remember feeling overwhelmed, so I often left school and went home when my parents were at work.

If a child is sent to a special school for children who cannot learn, how is this going to help a child who can learn, no matter how slow that learning process may take? I am a slow learner because I am dyslexic, but with the right teaching, support, and time, I will learn. As mentioned above, I used to recite my times tables when I was going to the mainstream school and when I went to the ESN school, I could devise and structure a play and remember my lines to perform it without even writing it down. Does this sound like a child who is backward? What is a backward child? They don't exist and they never did.

In my 40s, although I lacked many skills I should have learnt in school, I still graduated from university. I became a graduate because I had a 'brain that worked'. I later completed three more degrees. An adult who has severe learning difficulties could not have achieved all this, but they could still achieve with modern technology, patience and enough support in the classroom. No one deserves to be deliberately intellectually suppressed and be 'forced' to stay at the very bottom of the social hierarchy.

It is immoral to decide which child should climb the social hierarchy regardless of their potential abilities and qualities just because of their class, race, intellectual abilities. Not all are meant to clean the streets. If that was the case, who would design the cleaning tools? Who would invent the cleaning substances to used to clean our environment in order to prevent the spread of diseases? And who would entertain the people and govern the country?

Oh, I forgot! The British government already had its professionals and leaders, but following the Second World War, Britain lacked labourers to help rebuild its crushed economy. And, of course, it could always rely on black people from its colonies to come, along with their children, to help.

And so, with the help of the British Education System, before my children and I were born, the British government decided that we should be cleaners or work in a factory, even if it was our desire, or even destiny, to work in other areas of society, where we could earn a good salary to help our families have a better lifestyle. I was used as a guinea pig to create a dynasty for my children to inherit, as Bernard Coard predicted.

IT TAKES A WHOLE VILLAGE TO RAISE A CHILD: (MY ENGLISH RACIST TEACHERS)

It was a secret among the white, middle-class teachers that black children would fail IQ assessments even if their intelligence was above average. Thereafter, to please the English working-class parents, they sent black children to special schools out of their area on special buses.

However, unfortunately for them, Bernard Coard discovered their shocking racist secret through thorough investigation, and he exposed them in a book he wrote entitled: How the West Indian Child Is made Educationally Sub-normal in the British School System.

Bernard came from Grenada to Britain to do a master's degree. Between the summer of 1967 and December 1970, he ran evening clubs for seven schools for the educationally subnormal, before teaching full-time at two other ESN schools. Bernard writes: "This gave me first-hand experience of what was happening not just in these schools but in the education system as a whole" (Coard, p. 56).

What if I lived in the same city as Bernard, and he was my teacher? I would have left school being able to read and write, and I wouldn't have had a story to share with the world. I would have gone on to study Performing Arts, worked as an actress and in later life become a politician. Most importantly, my children would have had a great life; we would have travelled the world together. If only!Bernard's book created a discourse among both professionals and West Indian parents about black children being put into special schools regardless of their intelligence, which led to the setting up of Saturday schools in West Indian communities to teach black children.

The Caribbean community will be forever indebted to this great man. It was this discourse that prompted my mother to take me to a child psychologist who was also a social worker. She game me a professional assessment and helped me to go to a mainstream school. Although this helped me, it was far too late.

> *Tanky kyaan buy bread*
> *Kind words alone are not enough,*
> *they need to be supported by action*
> *Everal McKenzie*

I will forever be thankful to Bernard Coard.

Here is a poem I have written in pure,

eternal gratitude to this wonderful and beautiful man.

The Thunders Opened Their Jaws and Roared The Name Bernard Coard

All the way in Grenada in the Caribbean

There lived an intelligent young man

Whose destiny was not in his homeland

But across the ocean under foreign clouds

He will go to name and to shame

the colonising proud.

IT TAKES A WHOLE VILLAGE TO RAISE A CHILD: (MY ENGLISH RACIST TEACHERS)

By the mighty hands of the Holy Divine

He was placed in the midst of a maze with a sign

Only he had the mind and the eyes to discern,

And thereafter wave a flag of great concern,

He declared 'a deceitful foul-play'

That only he could unravel straight a way

Who is this man? They say,

Bernard Coard is his name

And his fame

He revealed the plight of the West Indian child

did Coard

In a cold and hostile country he record

How they made them educationally subnormal

And thrown into a dustbin school for eternal.

"You are going to a new school" said my mother

I was shocked and started to cry

"I don't want to leave", I desperately uttered

And I began to sob and sob and sob,

SUBNORMAL

when I felt a mighty blow to my back

It was only my dad's saying shut up

"No crying in my house."

Like the slave master would announce

On the plantation afraid,

my shy mother looked on until

I stood absolutely still

I took a deep, deep, breath in

Crying was not his thing

As the wave of sadness filled my skin

And touched my aching heart

when his wicked hands depart

Who cares about the black child

A man called Bernard Coard

What he discovered was chilling to the bone

How the black child was being groomed alone

Labelled as being backward, dull and inferior

Destined to spend the rest of their days

as a mere labourer

IT TAKES A WHOLE VILLAGE TO RAISE A CHILD: (MY ENGLISH RACIST TEACHERS)

Poor wages, housing, and no motivation, bound

To have offspring with similar background

And so it was predicted by the year two thousand

There would be a Black helot class in English towns

Lurking about like serfs and slaves no doubt

They made me into an introvert

While deep inside I was overtly loud and alert

A creative child an entertainer, a writer

An activist, a campaigner

A brave child,

they made tremble

and weaker

When my mother heard the discourse

About the publication of Bernard's book, of course

She took me to a black child's psychologist

There I learnt a new word I didn't know exist

You are intelligent she said

I knew it was something good in my head

She turned and looked at me

SUBNORMAL

God sanctify you Bernard Coard

With you, no child can ever perish

Children of all colours is the rainbow in your sky

A great man, who educates

A great man, who save lives not takes

A great man, words cannot describe

A great man, I'm bewildered and floored by your charms

A great man, with outstanding pure good vibes

Your memory will forever be cherished,

when the thunders open their jaws

and roar

the name

Bernard Coard

African Proverbs

Train a child the way he should go

and make sure you also go the same way.

Respect a little child,

and let it respect you.

Bantu Proverb

I would often wake up to find a mysterious, dark, towering figure standing over my bed like a dream. When I saw this dark shape amid pure darkness,

it took me awhile to discern who it was because I feared the dark

and I would have thought it was a ghost.

By this time,

my heart was thumping loudly, and I was trembling uncontrollably.

However, within seconds, I knew it was my father standing over me with one hand in the air,

about to strike me in my sleep.

Chapter Five

It Takes a Whole Village to Raise a Child: (My Colonial Family)

The ancient African proverb 'It Takes a Whole Village to Raise a Child' is a powerful truth. Parents who believe they raise their children alone are naïve because everyone your child comes into contact with can influence their lives in one way or another.

In the previous chapter, I talked about my English teachers who made me educationally subnormal, although as professionals, they knew I had the ability to learn, but they wanted to design a future for me and change my destiny for the worse to suit themselves.

This chapter narrates the part of my story where my family, mostly my father and other relatives, also helped to mould and shape me in a way that prevented me from functioning normally in society. First, my parents agreed for me to go to a special school. They could have told the teachers that they didn't want their daughter to be labelled as having special needs. They could have insisted on me staying at the mainstream school. There were parents who sent their children back to the West Indies to go to school because they realised that British education was inferior to the education in the Caribbean. Instead, my parents allowed me to go to an SEN school, while at home they made me a nervous little girl who would forever be looking for love and acceptance. Though to be fair to my parents, like most parents, when they heard the word special, they probably thought I would receive the best education because many believed that the education was superior in Britain.

When black families came to Britain after the Second World War, they derived from a patriarchal culture that was identical to the family structure of the slave societies throughout the Americas. This family structure was still apparent throughout Europe when West Indians came to England after the war. Men had always been at the forefront of all areas in society. Very few men would allow their wives to make decisions with them and very few men would become involved in domestic chores because such chores were seen as part of a woman's role. The man was both the head and owner of the house, even if both of them worked to buy the house.

It is a common belief that Africa was mostly a patriarchal society. However, this was not an accurate account of African society before European invasions of Africa. During the times of the European conquest in Africa, (including Egypt which was first colonised by Ethiopians) starting with the Persians and Romans, they were overcome with amazement to discover that women were equal to men and they both fought in wars side by side. African family structure was matriarchal and both men and women worked as domestic labourers, whereas in the western world, it was patriarchal. In some tribes, women could even have more than one husband, which was unheard of in Europe right up to today.

After the abolition of slavery, free societies in the Caribbean would have been identical to European societies in terms of how women and children were treated. In England, women were abused

IT TAKES A WHOLE VILLAGE TO RAISE A CHILD: (MY COLONIAL FAMILY)

and treated as second class well into the 1900s; an epoch that witnessed the birth of the suffragette movement in 1903, when women burnt their bras as they protested in the streets for equality and their right to vote. Before this period, women could not vote, just like Roman women, who also had no voice. And thus, unlike African society before the invasion of Europeans, the Caribbean social structure was almost identical to English a patriarchal society where men are at the forefront of all areas in society.

My father was from this epoch. He was born in 1908 during a time when wives obeyed their husbands and children were seen and not heard, or they would get a flogging. He was a very proud man who worked hard and didn't ask anyone for anything. He often said that when he died, he didn't want to be indebted to anyone, but people could owe him because it was between them and their God. I have taken on his philosophy and, like my father, I will be free of debts before I leave this world.

He wasn't a tall man or large built. He was just over average height for a man and had a dark, golden-brown complexion. I remember a friend asking me his age, and I honestly said he was nearly a hundred, although he would have been in his mid-fifties. He had a lazy eye that looked cross all the time; because he was a quick-tempered man, you could see the anger in that eye. He walked with a slight limp, so I used to think he was in pain. The fact was that one of his legs was shorter than the other, and he had big, flat feet. When my mother was on her deathbed I showed my soul-friend my father's passport picture, and she said he was handsome. But he wasn't handsome to me because if he was, I would have been much better looking

Mum was a very beautiful lady and, like dad, her skin was the colour of copper, but a little darker; with beautiful, grey cat eyes, soft, high cheekbones, soft, wavy African hair, and she was an average height for a woman. When comparing her to dad, who I described as an angry lion, I always said she was like a mouse, but then, I would ask, can you catch a mouse easily? Mum had a gentle soul, though she wasn't as gentle as she appeared to be. Mother was a brave soul, although very, very shy. She spoke very softly and would often lean her head to one side like Diana, Princess of Wales while she did so.

My mother's siblings may disagree with me, but I can only write about what my mother told me. She said that she was her father's favourite. She loved sitting on the floor between his legs when she was a very young child. She described her mother as extremely beautiful with very dark, comely skin. Apparently, my grandfather was interested in two young ladies but he chose my grandmother because she was quiet, whereas the other lady was very loud.

Like my dad, my mother was a woman of her time; an obeying, nurturing wife who took her wifely duties very seriously, although she wasn't afraid to stand up to her husband sometimes. She cooked for him, kept the house clean and massaged him, especially when he had muscle pain. Everything was in its place in the house. There was never a moment when I saw a pile of clothes in the wash room waiting to be washed. When the clothes were washed, they were put to dry immediately and then ironed. Dishes were washed and never left in the sink. I cannot remember the house being dirty or untidy and dad certainly didn't do any housework, being a man of his time, and she never asked me to help her, which she should have done because when I became a teenager, she couldn't get me to do anything in the

IT TAKES A WHOLE VILLAGE TO RAISE A CHILD: (MY COLONIAL FAMILY)

house. Throughout my childhood, there was no structure either at school or at home so I have a lazy attitude to life.

As I mentioned in the introduction, my mother came from a middle-class background. Her father owned five plantations, which he must have inherited from his white grandfather, whereas my dad owned only a few acres of land. My mother's father was a deacon, and he used to send money to Africa.

When my mum passed away, her nephew told me that granddad wasn't a good man because he was half white, but he was the perfect father to my mother and that is what counts. At least he was a better father than my mother's nephew and my father – he petrified me. My mother's nephew is a father to biracial children, so I do not know what he meant by that statement; your race has nothing to do with your character.

As for my father, he could never fill the footsteps of my grandfather, who nurtured his daughter (my mother). I would often wake up to find a mysterious, dark, towering figure standing over my bed like a nightmare. When I saw this dark shape amid pure darkness, it took me a while to discern who it was because I feared the dark and I would have thought it was a ghost. By this time, my heart was thumping loudly, and I was trembling uncontrollably. However, within seconds, I knew it was my father standing over me with one hand in the air, about to strike me in my sleep. I must have done something wrong, as children normally do, the day before, and he couldn't catch me to beat me there and then because as soon as I knew I was in trouble, I ran out of the house.

He had in his hand either a belt, my mother's stiletto high-heel shoes, the iron cord, or a rubber [implement] he called a cow-cod that he had got from work especially to beat me with. He just knew that one day he would beat me, so he had prepared for it. Sometimes my mother came to my rescue, although she knew he would hit her, too. There were times when she was down in the kitchen making breakfast and didn't hear me crying. This would be in the early hours of the morning before he went to work. He left the house about 5 a.m., so mum woke up to make his breakfast around 4 a.m.

I have to be honest, sometimes I deserved punishment; but not like that. I am so happy that some parents today find other alternative ways to punish their children without using violence. I wouldn't like to find out that my precious grandson is flogged like I was. I was just a child who needed love and praise from her parents, which I wasn't getting a school. Young children spend their time trying to familiarise themselves with the world they find themselves in. We often do the wrong things, and our parents are supposed to love us and teach us with love, but I was constantly getting beaten. My skin was always battered and sore.

I was forever running away from my dad, even after he died; for about ten years, I was running away from him in my dreams. I was also afraid that I would wake up one night and see his spirit standing over my bed but, thank God, that never happened. Perhaps because I was always getting punished by my father, my mother never punished me. She never hit me! In saying all this, mum very rarely spoke to me, like my teachers. No one was talking to me; no wonder it took me a life time to develop language skills. My big sister also never, ever spoke to me, so I saw myself as being an only child. I was so unhappy and lonely and most of the time I just wanted to get out of that house.

I didn't like food. I preferred bulla cake and bananas or chocolate and sweets, so I often stole the change out of my father's jacket pocket that was hanging on the door to go to the shop because I was hungry. He had so many coins in his pocket, I never thought he would miss a few of them; he probably didn't miss them. Looking back on it now, I didn't realise that he could see me through the mirror of my mother's dressing table. So, he must have got his kicks out of watching me dipping my hands into his pocket, knowing that, one day, he would catch me when I least expected it and beat the living daylights out of me.

My father grew up in a British colonial patriarchal world, where children were seen and not heard, and it wasn't against the law to beat your child, or even your wife, in England. Most Caribbean children from these times will remember getting beatings, but some parents went too far, as is always the case. As I mentioned previously, in a society like this, the men were at the forefront of everything, and women were submissive and treated as second-class citizens. They were derived from an epoch where English men could sell their wives instead of divorcing them right up until the 1840s. As for the children, they were supposed to be seen and not heard, apart from when they were screaming because they were being flogged like slaves.

On one occasion, I am not sure what I did; he was whipping me with the cow-cod he kept under the mattress. Sometimes my mother would take it and throw it in the bin, but he would only bring another one from work. The cow-cod was either black or grey and it was very thick. When you placed it on a flat surface, it would curl up. I think it was dad who gave it its name because I've done research on this cow-cod, and I couldn't find anything with that name. However, later, I discovered that cow-cod soup is made with a bull's penis, so that's where the name came from. Also, rockfish species is called cow cod.

As I was saying, he was beating me and while he was doing so, he often asked me to tell him his name. "Who am I?" he shouted in pour madness, as he looked down on his little bony fragile child. There was no mercy in his eyes, especially in his lazy angry eye. He wanted me to tell him his name or that he was "daddy" like Kunta Kinte in Roots, when he was whipped by the slave master who would make him say his new slave name "Toby". While this was going on, the young African man who rented the living room came upstairs to pay his rent. When he saw the way my dad was beating me, he was very concerned and politely asked my dad not to beat me like that. My dad left me and walked towards him and started beating him with the cow-cod. I couldn't run because they were at the door or else I would have escaped and jumped from the top of the stairs to the bottom, and run right out of the house, like I normally did. Who knows, maybe that would have been the day my parents would have seen me for the last time because I was so afraid. I just could not believe that he was beating the young man. At the time, I would have been about eight years old. As for the African man, he moved out that same week.

Sometimes my dad abused me for no reason, and he did it in a hateful, inhuman way, as if I was his slave, and he was my master. It was a tradition in our home that once a year my dad cooked cow foot. That was the only time dad went to the kitchen, unless he was going to fix something or do decorating. While cooking, he tasted the food, and I could tell by his face that he was pleased, so I asked him politely if I could taste it too. He shouted at me. He then picked me up and turned me upside down, carried me over to the wall and started banging me on the wall like a dirty mat while I was still upside down. My mother screamed out and placed her hands on her head, before she leapt over to him. She touched him so he would put me down, but it was as though he was in a trance and he kept banging me on the wall. Afterwards, I remember shaking and crying and forcing myself not to cry because if I dared to cry, he would just pick me up and do it all over again.

My father made me so nervous that in my late teens my hands used to still shake, despite the fact that by then he would have been dead for around five years. I remember my cousin's husband asking me why my hands trembled so much. I didn't answer because I couldn't connect the shaking to my dad because, after he died, I blocked him out of my memory.

My body trembled for days after he bashed me against the wall. I was always nervous, and still am nervous, but I am healing. I was a dyslexic child who was having my body bashed against the wall, only to go to school in the morning to be taught a subnormal education. It is a miracle that I am writing this book. It is also a miracle that I was never admitted to a mental hospital though I have been depressed nearly all of my life.

While my dad was bashing my body against the wall, and holding me upside down by my legs, as if I was a wooden bat, my poor mum couldn't do anything. If she had dared to try, he would have dropped me on the floor like a ball and started to beat her up, too. All this had happened because I asked him if I could taste his stupid, unseasoned disgusting cow-foot!

When I grew up, I reminded mum about the time dad did this to me, but she said that he did it several times. I must have blocked it from my mind and buried it in my subconscious, because I could only remember him doing it once, which was more than enough.

He also used to barge into the bathroom, when I was just about to get into the bath, to scrub me down with a rough scrubbing brush, like the ones ladies used to use in the 1920s to scrub their clothes and the floor. The skin on my body rose like the ocean waves; it was red and swollen. I would just sit in the bath and cry after he had gone; asking myself "why, what did I do?" I honestly thought my dad hated me because I was an ugly and very thin child with a tiny face.

Throughout my childhood and until I was in my mid-thirties, whenever there was thunder and lightning, I would get out of bed and go to the toilet and close the door. I never knew why I did this, but when I discovered why, I was never afraid again, thanks to my cousin.

My cousin came to see me. He used to live in our house when he was a child. We briefly spoke about those days. He told me he remembered once when I went out on my own, as I normally did, and my dad told everyone in the house not to open the door on my return. On the way back, it was thundering; the rain was pelting down, and the lightning lit up the afternoon sky. When my dad gave an order, no one dared to disobey him or else there would be a big argument and the tenants might have to leave. If my mother opened the door for me, she would get a beating. I used to say that even the ghosts were afraid of my dad. When the tenants in our house complained about seeing ghostly shadows, my dad used to tell them to send them to him, he would deal with them, but the ghosts never allowed my dad to see them.

Perhaps he didn't want anyone to open the door because he was angry that I'd gone out without his permission. I used to go out because I was trying to escape a beating or maybe I just needed fresh air; I always felt uncomfortable in that house. The house was strange, with thick, negative vibes, and I was very sensitive to it all. Or perhaps I would go out because I didn't feel like watching the television in his room and watching him masturbate, or to avoid a beating for not realising that he'd finished eating and I'd not taken his plate to the kitchen, because I was watching the television and I hadn't realised he'd finished. I would only know that he had finished when our eyes met and I suddenly realised, but by this time, I would have had to run away as fast as I could to avoid a beating, although I knew he would catch me when I least expected it in the early hours of the morning.

As I have already mentioned, sometimes, when it was just dad and I in the room, he would sit there and masturbate in front of me. Yet the strange thing is, I never told my mother, even when I became an adult. Perhaps, subconsciously, I wanted to protect her because she didn't deserve to hear such horrible news about what her husband was doing in front of me. Though I probably wouldn't have said anything, whether she deserved to know or not, because of the need to protect both my parents. I will never understand the psychology behind children having a desperate need to protect their parents, even when they know they are bad people, like my dad, although people who didn't really know him would have disagreed with me. He was bad to me but his friends loved him and enjoyed his company when they came to the house to see him or when he went out with them to the pub. He often entertained them and made them laugh, but when they left the house there was no laughter between mum, dad and me. However, there was plenty between him and his friends.

When my dad's friends came over, he would buy them whisky and his friends would sit me on their knees and feel my private parts. Perhaps he couldn't see them because they always sat behind him, but he knew I was in the room, so why didn't he look to see if I was okay?

Dad's friends weren't the only ones who used to abuse me sexually. He used to employ an English man to help him to decorate his house and this man often tried to penetrate me. When I became sexually active, sex was very painful because of this, until I had my third child when I was twenty-seven years old. In retrospect, it is no wonder that I didn't want to be in that house.

My haunted house I once hated but grew up to love. Yes, you read correctly, and no, I didn't have hallucinations as a child. I will narrate this part of the book with some evidence of living in a hunted house, although you might not believe me, anyway.

Like a lot of children, I was afraid of the dark. I hated my curtains drawn together at night. Looking back now, I don't know why I didn't just get up and draw them back when mum had closed them. So I just lay there petrified, unable to fall asleep.

When we first moved in, I used to go into my parents' room because of a strange noise I used to hear almost every night between the ages of five and ten. It was difficult to determine exactly what the noise was, but when I got older, I could only describe the noise as drums beating simultaneously together. The sound started at the bottom of the stairs on the ground floor and became louder as it got closer to my room on the first floor. Thereafter, the noise continued up the next flight of stairs towards my big sister's room on the second floor, before descending back to where it started from. This continued throughout the night until it finally stopped, when I would finally try to sleep.

It was also difficult to wake up in the mornings, and bed was the last thing on my mind at bedtime. The thought of hearing this horrible sound for yet another night made my heart leap into my throat and already, at five years old, I was having panic attacks when I would tremble inside.

On nights I didn't hear the noise, I would suddenly wake up with the ghostly feeling that someone was there in the room. At first, I thought it was my mum, but I realised it couldn't have been her. I peeped through a hole that I had made in the sheets and, to my horror, I saw a soldier standing in front of my mother's sewing machine. He was a young, white man in a uniform, just staring down at me. His dreamy, weary transparent eyes pierced mine, so I immediately covered my head. But with the sound of my heavy breathing, and my heart beat pounding away, there was no way I was going to sleep.

When I was a very young child, my parents would wake up to find me sleeping between them. As I got older, I told my parents about the noises and the white soldier who kept coming into my room. My father discovered that our house was used as a hospice for dying and wounded soldiers during World War Two. This explained the apparition of the soldier in my room. As for the sound of drums, this was actually soldiers marching up and down the stairs. It also explained why we had bells on the walls in our house.

The white soldier wasn't the only ghost in our house that liked my company. The energies in our house were many, and I felt them all. Though I felt so alone, I was not alone. There were other people and children in our house apart from us and the tenants, but no one could see them except me. There was always someone near me. I felt the energies against my back as I walked through the house.

One day, I was going to the kitchen in the basement when I saw an Indian lady with enormous eyes, a round face and long black hair standing in the corner of the hallway. I was so shocked; the first time I saw her I ran out of the house. I saw her several times just walking through the house as though she lived with us.

One night, I had a strange feeling that someone had just walked into my room. My back was facing the door while in bed. I thought it was the soldier, so I was just going to ignore him and try to sleep when I felt something against my back, so I turned over to see what was there. As I turned over, I saw a little Indian boy fall off my bed. When I looked at the floor, he vanished before my very eyes. I can even remember what he was wearing. He wore a striped red and white tee-shirt. I was so very shocked; I felt my head getting bigger and bigger and I could hear my heart beating in my ears. It was a living nightmare I was experiencing while awake. From that moment on, I always laid across the bed so that he couldn't get into bed with me

IT TAKES A WHOLE VILLAGE TO RAISE A CHILD: (MY COLONIAL FAMILY)

again and I would tuck the sheets around me, to stop him from getting underneath them. When I woke up the next morning, I had wet my bed. I never saw him again, but I knew he was there, lying next to me.

Just in case you think I was hallucinating, I wasn't the only one to see apparitions in the house. However, I was the only one who saw apparitions that looked like actual people. The family that lived in the basement used to complain about a black and grey shadow moving about near the light switch when suddenly the light went on and off. I experienced this apparition all the time.

As I got older, while I was cooking fried eggs and bacon, I would suddenly turn around because I felt someone watching me. As soon as I turned to look, the light in the hallway would turn off, and there was no one there, only a black or greyish, whitish shadow hovering in the air before quickly moving into the next room. It happened so many times, I would just open the kitchen door to the back garden and continue to do what I was doing, but this didn't mean that I wasn't afraid. I felt safer when the door was open, as I could hear people outside and the birds singing.

Most of the tenants saw shadows in our house, including my mother's cousin who rented a room with her three children. It was one of her sons who told me that I was afraid of thunder and lightning because dad refused to let me in during a thunderstorm. Well, his mother also used to see the curtains moving about. The only one who didn't see apparitions was my father, and he was very jealous of us. He wondered why they didn't appear to him so that he could swear at them and tell them to leave his house. So, he really thought that everyone was hallucinating, and he just laughed at us. But for me, it was no joke. I detested that house because of all that was happening there. I was delighted when my father sold it, to return to Jamaica, when I was nearly fourteen years old.

But there were good times at home, too. I don't believe there is any situation that is completely bad. My aunty used to say, "out of bad must come good". The most pleasant time for me (although not so pleasant for my parents) was when my parents argued, and then sometimes mum would sleep with me. You can never imagine how at peace I was on those nights. Mum's presence made me feel relaxed, and I felt no fear or loneliness. I'd curl up next to mum like a little kitten. The next morning, it was easy to wake up, because I had slept all the way through the night, but that didn't happen often.

In the '60s, most Caribbean people went to Blackpool for their holidays. In the front room of nearly every Caribbean home, there were Blackpool souvenirs. We also went to Blackpool, as a family, but not very often. But whenever there was a family or a friend's christening, we were there. I guess, because dad was a sociable man and kind to his friends, they wanted him to be the godfather to their children. It is a possibility that he lived up to his obligations, because I remember him buying shirts for my mother's little nephew, who was three years younger than me, and who he loved very much. He always said he loved boy children more than girls. He was very nice to my little cousin I told you about, the one who made me realise why I was afraid of thunder and lightning, but then he was a good little boy and never got into trouble unlike me. As a child, I was a dreamer, courageous, creative, inquisitive, bold and courageous, confident, and independent. In my opinion, I was an in-your-face type of child. I played with all my neighbours' children, and I was always in their houses. I would never allow myself to experience boredom though I didn't have a lot of toys.

As a family, we also went to weddings where, ironically, they chose dad to be the master of ceremonies, where he would give a speech about how a man should treat his wife, although he often beat his own wife. We also used to travel to other cities in England to visit families; they used to visit us, too. There would be plenty of laughter because dad knew how to entertain his guests.

Twenty years after we moved out of the family house in 1972, I began having dreams about going back there. Though I was dreaming, miraculously, I could see that the family living in our house had made changes, although I never saw them in my dreams. The house looked different every time and I was the only one walking around like a ghost, roaming from room to room. The atmosphere was lifeless, and even my presence was transparent. There were no sounds. I couldn't even hear my footsteps or the sound of the doors as I closed them behind me, or feel the doorknob when I opened the door. I had no sense of touch, smell or fear, just loneliness, as I looked out of my bedroom window at my neighbours, where I used to play with my friends.

My parents were in my mind's eye as I reached out to touch them before they slowly faded away into nothingness. Looking out of the window in my old bedroom where I used to sleep as a child, I summoned my neighbours to draw closer to the window, so I could see them. I watched and waited and waited until I awoke from the dream. Was my energy now among the ghosts that haunted the house that I once lived as a child? Am I now the ghost they can see, the way I used to see them? Ironically, if I won the lottery, I would buy that house to use as a shelter for abused wives and their children. Though I hated the house as a child, it is a house I am now very fond of.

When I was about eleven or twelve years old, I was happy when my mother told me she was going to go to the Caribbean and I was going to live with my aunty in another city because my father couldn't look after me. At last, I was going to leave that house for the first time since I had moved there at three years old. I really wanted a break from both my parents and that house. It was a moment of great excitement.

My aunty and her husband used to visit us with their daughter, who was three months younger than me. Although my cousin didn't like me very much, I was still happy to live with them because I thought her father was the best father in the world. I used to dream about marrying a man who was a good father, like him, and about having a big family, so I would never be lonely again. However, going to live with them was like jumping out of a frying pan into a blazing fire. What do you expect from a family suffering from mental slavery, when they create an environment where children are seen and not heard, where the only punishment is a beating and name-calling is the norm?

I left an abusive, ghostly environment only to live in one that wasn't much better. I lived with them for about a year and during that time I was becoming more and more self-conscious, because my aunty used to abuse me verbally so much. The way she treated me made me wonder if she really loved my mother, who was her sister,

MEETING MY SOUL-FRIEND AND MY SOULMATE AND GOING TO COLLEGE

met someone very special. I had a very positive impression of him but, like many people, I wasn't sure if he was my soul-mate or not, but looking back if he was, I would have known.

They were about to show me the way to the hostel when the one who didn't speak any English said goodbye to me in French and crossed over the road. At this point, my daughter started crying. He asked why she was crying and I told him that she hadn't drunk her milk when we went to the café and she was hungry. He decided there and then to buy her milk, although I told him I had some in my bag. He wouldn't listen, so off we went to the shop to buy milk. On our way back, we stopped at a restaurant to eat; I couldn't believe it was dinnertime already. I really wanted to taste French pancakes, so that was what I chose on the menu. While he was ordering the food, I fed my daughter and she then fell asleep for at least two hours. When we finished eating, we just talked and talked. I'd never have guessed that I could have so much to say to a complete stranger who didn't speak much English. Until then, I'd been very reserved and said little to people I didn't know. But I felt like I had known this man forever. The more I talked, the more he became fascinated with me. He told me that I was the first black British girl he had ever met and because my parents were from the Caribbean, he used to call me Bob Marley's sister.

It was now too late for him to take me to the hostel because he had an appointment with the manager of the hostel where he was residing, but he promised to take me afterwards. As we got nearer to the building, I was shocked to discover it was right next door to the one I had just left. As a matter of fact, he had left his hostel five minutes before I had left mine that day, but he had seen his friend and stopped to talk to him, or else we would never have met. Talk about destiny! The hostel where he stayed was a part of the university that he was attending. He was studying to be a lawyer. I ended up staying with him in his room.

After he had introduced me to his friends, they often came to see me, even when he wasn't there. They took advantage of the opportunity to practise speaking English with me. I was exotic to them because I was Caribbean British, and I was the only person they knew from England.

With permission from the hostel's manager, I stayed with him for a whole month. We went everywhere together and sometimes with his friends. The only places we didn't go to together were clubs and pubs because he didn't have any female friends to babysit my daughter, but most of the time we stayed in anyway. He taught me some French before I started French lessons. He also began reading English-language books for foreign speakers, so he could teach me my own language. I never knew someone could learn so fast, but then I had been to a special school. He could speak several languages, when most Africans were just bilingual. He was also an excellent cook and taught me to make African stews. He was very kind to both me and my daughter. That was his nature, because he was also kind to his friends.

My soul-friend had told me that, in France, they spoke English, but of course that wasn't the reality when I arrived there. The reality was that, in school, they taught children English, but when you went shopping and to other public places, no one spoke English. I realised it was going to be difficult to find work. If I couldn't get a job in

England, how was I going to get work in a place where I didn't speak the language? And so my new friend, who by now was my boyfriend, suggested I could go to evening classes to learn French and work as an au pair, but I would have to take my daughter back home to live with my mother in England.

And so that was what I did. I went home and told mum that I had met this lovely man I liked and that I was going to study French and work as an au pair. Mum was very happy for me, but even more happy that my daughter was going to live with her.

When I went back to France, I enrolled on a French course. The students were from many parts of the world and they had to communicate in French. We couldn't greet each other in our own languages, so, right from the start, we had to learn to say hello and communicate in French. And interestingly, I was learning to do so. Possibly, I think, because there was a lot of repetition. We had to rewrite phrases and read out loud, which I had never done in the ESN school.

There were two parts to my plan: learning French and getting a job. I was learning French and enjoying it, but the second part wasn't happening. It was difficult to find au pair work, especially being black. It certainly didn't help that I also had a stutter and could hardly write or speak English properly.

My soulmate took me to many places to find work, but each time we were unsuccessful. My mother was helping me financially throughout this period. The reality was that I stood a far better chance of getting a job in England than in France; but we kept on trying. My boyfriend also helped me with my French homework, which was also improving his English as well as mine. He used to say that he could tell I hadn't had the right support at school, which was the reason I wasn't performing according to my level of intelligence and couldn't get a job. He actually asked me if I had even been to school! At the time, I didn't understand what he meant, because everyone goes to school in Europe unless they are home-schooled. Looking back now, I understand why he asked that question because you expect more from someone who went to school, even if they were not educated properly.

Our friendship had now blossomed into romance, but it was much more than a holiday romance. He had become a part of my destiny that would not end if I were to go back home. I knew he was going to make a significant difference in my life. I always felt safe, content and very happy in his presence and when I was away from him, I couldn't wait to for us to be together again.

One day, I suddenly had an overwhelming impulse to draw his portrait. He thought it was hilarious when I asked him to allow me to do it. Until then, I had never drawn anyone's portrait. I think I was trying to impress him. I made him laugh even more when I told him he reminded me of Muhammad Ali. As he chuckled away, I took his hands and led him towards the bed, where I gently made him sit down. I then began sketching his dark brown, round face. When it was time to draw his eyes, something extraordinary happened to me as I stared into his deep-set eyes. There was a mystifying blur that came over them, which made me feel uneasy and, since that moment, I felt something wasn't right. That same night I had the dream that foreign bugs were all over me. Foreign was the only name I could describe these creatures because I had never seen them before. But

MEETING MY SOUL-FRIEND AND MY SOULMATE AND GOING TO COLLEGE

Mother Nature didn't want me to see the future, because it had to be, I suppose.

After nearly a year of living in France, I still hadn't got a job, so I went back to England to live with my mother. I then discovered that I was pregnant. Though we were now living apart, our relationship was even stronger. One day, he came to visit us and promised my mother that he would always love and take care of me; a promise he would eventually break.

The year is 1985

I was now a mother of two, but I still lacked confidence. I had no experience and I couldn't even get a cleaning job. I found it difficult to apply for jobs; I had no references and struggled to fill out job application forms. I returned to London and stayed at my soul-friend's flat while my mother looked after my two children. By now, she was looking after four children and she loved it.

As always, my intention was to look for work. My soul-friend was also unemployed, so we both decided to search for a job together, which helped me. When I was sixteen, she helped me fill out the form to enrol on a course and now she was about to help me apply for my first job real job; without her help, I couldn't have done it. Out of the many hotel jobs we applied for, one hotel invited us for an interview and I was surprised that they had invited us both. Having my friend's help must have helped raise my confidence. We applied for different jobs, of course, in housekeeping. I applied for a chambermaid's job, while she applied for a Housekeeping Supervisor's role.

Anyway, we both got the jobs we had applied for, but she later discovered she was pregnant and left, while I stayed on. Basically, her role was to check the rooms after I had cleaned them, and she also did office work. Though it was a cleaning job, I liked the environment because it was a luxurious five-star hotel. I was responsible for cleaning fifteen rooms and I could work at my own pace, as long as I finished the rooms on time. I remember thinking the job was perfect for me, because I didn't have to work in a team and socialise with other people.

I was the first one to arrive at work, so I could pack my trolley with linen and enter the rooms of those guests who had checked out early. This way, I was always ahead of myself when it came to time. I had created a strategy to help me work more productively. When entering a room, I carried out the same routine every time, in order to build up speed and rhythm, which I'd been accused of not having when I was making the tea in the restaurant and was bullied as a result. By the way, I can't remember if I mentioned this before, but I didn't actually apply for that restaurant job; I just went in to enquire about the job and got it.

While I was working as a chambermaid, my mum was having difficulty taking care of my son, who was then nearly two years old. Mum said he was hyperactive, compared with my three-year-old daughter. I also thought that mum had enough on her plate for a lady in her mid-60s, looking after three children, so I asked my soul-friend if she could look after my son, since she was pregnant and wasn't working. She agreed, so I brought him to live with us and she took care of him while I went to work.

MEETING MY SOUL-FRIEND AND MY SOULMATE AND GOING TO COLLEGE

I was now travelling backwards and forwards between two cities, to visit my mother, and between England and France, where my soulmate lived. I was also travelling to other parts of Europe where his relatives lived. On other occasions, he travelled to stay with us at my soul-friend's flat, while I went to work. It must have been on such occasions that they became intimate.

Eventually, my soul-friend was offered a maisonette, so I stayed with her there while I was waiting for the council to offer me a place. However, before we moved to the maisonette, I was concerned that she was often reluctant to visit my mum to see her children or even to pay for childcare. We had arguments about this. I was more concerned that my mother was in her 60s, looking after her two children as well as my daughter, but my soul-friend didn't care. This was one of the reasons for taking my son back. After five years, I decided it was time that we both looked after our own children. She wasn't happy with the decisions I'd made and became very resentful towards me.

The children arrived before we moved to her new flat and it was obvious that she wanted us out as soon as possible. Sometimes, she refused to put on the hot water so I couldn't bath my children. Luckily, the council offered me a lovely three-bed maisonette. I was in the process of buying the essentials to move into the property, but she couldn't wait. So, we moved in and slept on the sofa until the beds arrived.

Now, I was focusing on making a loving, safe home for my family. I was hoping that, after my soulmate finished studying law, either he would move to England or we would both live in Africa, a place I have always dreamt of living in. We often discussed getting married in England and living there instead of in France. Before I gave birth to my third child, his second son, we romantically met in a hotel in Calais, where he got on one knee and asked me to marry him. I was over the moon and felt blessed. However, the moment was about to come when we would arrive at the crossroads of our relationship.

I always used to tell my fiancé that he could never be a king in another man's country. He used to laugh at me whenever I said this, although he agreed with me. And so, the time came when he was going back home to Africa. I was very sad and happy at the same time. I had always wanted to live in Africa, but I wanted us to go there together.

My baby was just three months old and at that time I wasn't ready to travel to Africa with my children and leave my mother because we had not planned such a journey. He had made a sudden decision to go there because his brother-in-law had secured a director's position in a company for my fiancé and they wanted him to start immediately. He had no choice but to travel. He didn't even have enough time to come to say goodbye to us, so I had to travel with my baby to see him before he left.

I was a bit late in boarding the plane and actually thought I was going to miss it and we wouldn't get the chance to say goodbye to him. I had a panic attack for the first time in my life. A member of the airport staff gave me some water to help calm down my nerves.

When I arrived at the family house, perhaps because he was overwhelmed with the fact that he was going back to Africa after so many years, he behaved coldly towards me. The last time he was in Africa

MEETING MY SOUL-FRIEND AND MY SOULMATE AND GOING TO COLLEGE

had been when he was a child. Anyway, I felt a distance between us, but I thought he was just excited that he was going home to Africa. He told me that the last time he was there was when he was ten years old. Looking back on it now, he was probably having doubts about our relationship but, like me, we couldn't see into the future. That strange feeling that I had after the dream about being covered in foreign bugs was also apparent in my mind, mixed with an uneasy feeling that he didn't want me around. He was so busy planning and talking to the family about the trip that he said very little to me. I just didn't have good feelings about him going away, but I couldn't discern the message that Mother Nature was trying to reveal to me, although it was actually loud and clear: he didn't love me any more. I really felt as though he no longer wanted our relationship, but then he asked me to tell mum to make my wedding dress, so I thought that maybe I was overreacting.

He assured me that, within a year, the children and I would join him, and then mum would come at a later date. Though he said all this, I still had a strange feeling haunting me whenever I thought of us being together, and it just wouldn't go away.

He kept his promise that we would join him. Within a year, the children and I joined him in Africa, but I only went there to cry a pool of tears. I returned home to England with a crushed heart and very disturbed. It took me ten years to get over my experience in Africa. Though I met the most beautiful and kindest people there, I'd simply been unlucky that I'd fallen in love with the wrong man and wasn't spiritual enough to listen when Mother Nature (the Universe) tried to warn me about him.

~ 145 ~

Because of my childhood, I was already depressed when I met him in France. He promised my mother he would make me happy, but no one can make you happy but yourself. So, the time came when I was starting to think more about loving myself and doing everything possible to improve my life.

At the time, the only thing that made me really happy was when I thought about learning to read and write properly, so I could educate myself. While I was in Africa, I made a pact with God that I was going to get my brain working if it killed me. What a promise to make to God, as a mother! Though it is a figure of speech, I still meant it. Who would have taken care of my children if I had died? My mother was 70 years old and I was an only child. I wasn't close to any of my cousins (sadly, this is still the case), so there would have been absolutely no one to take care of my children. However, my main priority now was to learn to read and write properly, not my children. Though I didn't realise it back then, that was what actually happened; I was so desperate to learn. I couldn't admit this when I first began writing my book. Whenever I remembered how I would prefer to die, rather than remain illiterate, I felt so guilty and ashamed that I stopped writing for several months, until I was strong enough to be honest with myself in order to narrate a true account of what really happened regarding my children.

Learning became a priority because I was dyslexic and made educationally subnormal. Therefore, I needed time to learn; time I could have spent working, paying for private lessons for my children and travelling the world with them, if only I hadn't been a product of an evil kind of racism very similar to slavery, where enslaved Africans remained at the very bottom of society and weren't allowed to read; in fact, it could be fatal for an enslaved African to be caught reading a book.

This is what being made educationally subnormal does to you; they try to turn you into a labourer slave hoping that your children will also be a labourers.

*If I thought for one second
that I would not have given my children
the best life,
I would not have brought them into this world.*

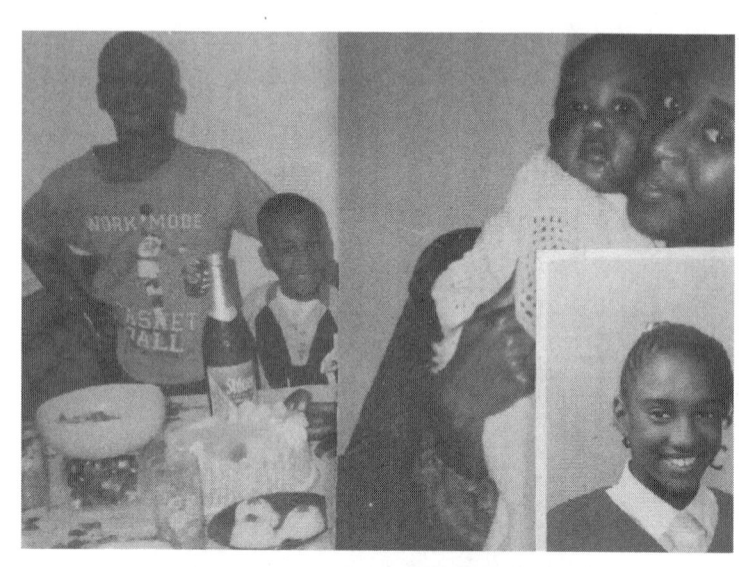

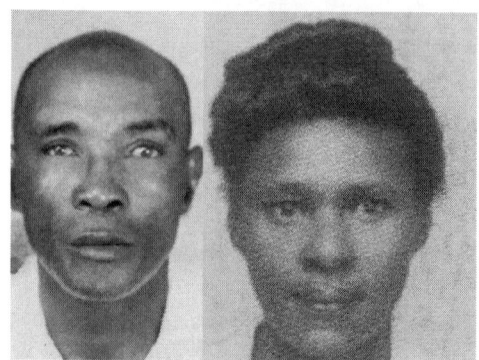

My Parents

Chapter Seven

How I Failed my Children Because The British Education System Failed Me

When the children and I arrived in England in December 1989, you can imagine how cold we were, considering we were not wearing any coats and were coming from one of the hottest countries in Africa.

I was so confident that I would never return to England once I had sent for my mother, that I had thrown away our coats when we were leaving. Even if I was going to return, it wouldn't be in the winter. As a symbolic gesture, I said out loud "Goodbye, Queen of England" because, being Caribbean British, I knew she would never have accepted me as one of her people; I just didn't look like them. Now, I was going to a country where people looked like me.

At the Tube station, my children were so cold that they were shivering like wet chickens. A white couple took off their coats and wrapped them around the children, but they took their coats back when we got into the train. I was talking with a friend about this what the couple did. My friend looked very serious, as though she was attempting to envisage the couple's goodwill gesture. Then she said, "Maisie, it was as though they were welcoming you home", and I agreed.

Leaving Africa, I didn't even realise it was nearly Christmas until I arrived in England. So I was so surprised to see how beautifully the

Christmas lights illuminated the city, along with the alluring, colourful trimmings. There were people rushing in and out of busy, rich-looking shops, carrying fat bags filled with useless things. And the hymns of the Salvation Army echoing endlessly through the frozen air was a delight to my ears at the station. My children's faces were lit up like Christmas trees; it was as though we had never been here before.

We were coming from a world where people couldn't even afford to buy a birthday cake for their children, let alone Christmas decorations for their homes. Even the English streets shone as brightly as the silver stars in the heavens, compared to the dusty, sandy roads that I had walked on for nearly a year. Africa had turned into a living hell, because the man I went there to marry changed his mind and wouldn't walk the road with me.

However, this rich, English city meant nothing to me, because I knew how England had come by its wealth. So, as I walked these shiny, clean streets, I was still reflecting on what I had left behind in Africa. What could have been. If only. If only he had really been my soulmate!

We arrived at my mother's flat late in the evening. I couldn't wait to knock on her door. As she opened it, within seconds, she gasped for breath. Mum's jaw dropped as sheer excitement, joy and spread across her face; and her grey, cat eyes became as big as those of an owl. As soon as she could catch her breath, my 70-year-old mother picked me up while I was still holding my baby in my arms. It wasn't difficult to pick me up, because I was skin and bone, and my baby had more worms in him than meat on his body.

Though it was late, mum still cooked chicken and rice with mashed potatoes for the children. We drank plenty of clean water and fresh milk; not even a calf would have enjoyed cow's milk like we did. From then on, when bathing, I noticed we were putting on weight every day.

On the Monday, we went to the doctor for worm medicine and vitamins. And thus, the healing began, but we had far to go to get over the trauma I had gone through in Africa. As for the children, they were too young to realise what had happened. Though the healing had begun, the future looked bleak without my children's father; we needed him. And from that moment, guilt haunted every part of my being; I had failed my children and lost their father.

We couldn't stay at my mum's place for long, so the following week I went to the council to apply for accommodation. My appointment was with a black British lady and when she heard my story, it brought tears to her eyes. Afterwards, she made me a cup of tea and left me alone in the room for nearly an hour. When she eventually came back, her red, tearful eyes had now resumed their normal colour. She had a pleasant smile on her face. She walked straight towards me with a bunch of keys in her hand, placed them in my right hand and pressed all my fingers down on top of them. With a soft voice, like a Samaritan trying to persuade a caller not to commit suicide, she said, "This is for you", with much pride in her large, brown eyes. All I could say was "thank you", with a grateful smile and a relieved heart. They were the keys to a three-bedroom house with a large garden. It was only temporary until they found me a permanent place.

I couldn't wait to go home and tell mum. Everything in the house was new. The carpet, washing machine, cooker and kitchenware were all new. Even the plastic covers were still on the beds and toys were in their packaging. We moved into the house just before Christmas Day.

Before Christmas, I also found a school for my eldest two children and a nursery for my two yearold. My eldest son went to a church school in Africa, but it not for long because he was too hyperactive and they couldn't control him. The pastor was only helping me out of charity because he knew I could not pay the school fees, so only one of my children could go.

Now we were back home in England, my son was about to start school for the first time with his sister. The school was about five minutes' walk from my mother's flat, and would be less than ten minutes' walk from my temporary accommodation once we left my mother's place. My baby boy went to a nursery from 10 a.m. until 3 p.m.. After leaving him, I would go to the Samaritans because I needed to talk. I really needed to talk then and I still can't stop talking. As I have said previously, I am hoping that when this book is published, I can at last put my past behind me for ever.

Though I had always had problems communicating with others because I had a small vocabulary and was always sad, my experience in Africa had made these problems worse. I was traumatised and this had affected my mind as well as my ability to converse with people I knew well without forgetting the point I was making or acknowledging what they were saying to me. If I was making a cup of tea and had to go off and do something else, on my return I would forget what I had done and make another cup of tea. I was only thirty years old. Going to the Samaritans helped me get used to communicating again, especially in English.

One of the things I talked about at the Samaritans was being a single mother. I hated the idea of being a single mother. I was convinced that a healthy home depended on two good parents. As always, I had my mother to help me, but she was now nearly seventy-one years old and slowing down a little. However, she was always there for me. I now also had the school to help me because, unlike in the African country I had been in, education in England was free and mandatory.

While my children were at school from 9 a.m. to 3.30 p.m. and my youngest was at nursery, with the help of the Samaritans I could heal and plan my life because we talked about the future, too.

I also went to a Relate counsellor who normally counselled married couples, but when my story was heard, I was allowed to attend a few sessions. However, I preferred to go to the Samaritans because I could talk for nearly four hours, if I wanted to, whereas at Relate, it was only a twenty-minute session, which wasn't enough for me.

It never occurred to me that perhaps my two eldest children, at five and eight years old, would benefit from having counselling, like me. Nor did I ever think about how the entire ordeal in Africa had affected them. In Africa, they could play all the time and I always made sure they had food, even if I had to go without myself. My daughter had two girls who came to play with her and two boys, who were twins, came to play with my son. Although they played as children, the fact is that I was very depressed in Africa because of my unfortunate situation, so they would have known that "mummy is sad" and this would have made them sad, too but, like all children, they wouldn't have known how to express their feelings, so they just continued to play.

After leaving the Samaritans, I would rush to get my baby from the nursery while my mother collected my two eldest from school. But going home was depressing. While I poured out my heart to the lady at the Samaritans, I was dealing with memories that were painful and made me cry, but at least there were just images in my mind. At home, however, there was hysteria and chaos that I had to deal with, and I was too depressed and depleted in strength to deal with so many things at the same time every day. I was very depressed and became even more depressed trying to raise my children alone that I had chosen to bring into this world. I don't know why I was like this. Other single parents manage to bring up their children but, for me, I needed more help than my mother could give me at the time. She had done enough already.

My eldest child is my daughter. She was becoming more and more reserved. When she was five years old, she wasn't talking and was hardly eating anything, even from when she was a toddler. I knew something wasn't right, but I couldn't put my finger on it. I thought she might be partly deaf and blind, so I took her to have her ears and eyes tested. Her hearing was fine, but she needed glasses.

My daughter began talking to herself as if she had an invisible friend. I often went to the school at playtime to watch her play, but I went home feeling even more upset to see her playing in isolation, talking to herself and making gestures with her hands, as though she was talking to someone. Her eyes looked as though she was blind to her surroundings; she was in a world of her own.

I am so ashamed, but I must confess to you and my daughter that I used to get upset with her for raising her hands while she walked. Being an ignorant mother, always aiming for perfection, I would order her (in a stern, aggressive voice) to put her arms down, but she continued doing so for a few years, until she was about eleven, when she finally stopped. I hated to see anything that was abnormal. I didn't like myself because I thought I didn't look normal. Also, I guess I was reacting more like my father would have done; my mother wouldn't have reacted this way, if I was walking with my arms up in the air. Mum wouldn't have said anything. She would have just allowed me to grow out of it in my own time.

Sadly, none of the children at school played with my daughter. They said she was weird, and they bullied her. I asked to have a meeting with both the teacher and the headteacher, because I would not tolerate my child being bullied, but they did nothing, despite visiting the school several times to talk with them. They always had a smirk on their faces when I complained about my daughter being bullied. Her disengaged body language said it all; she just wasn't interested in what I was saying.

Still unable to read or write properly, as I had not yet attended college, I didn't have the words to communicate effectively with the school, on behalf of my children, and I wasn't as assertive then as I am today. My children and I needed help, but who was going to help a young, black family in the early '90s? The children needed more help than I could give them. If we had been a close family, that would have helped; but that had never been the case and still isn't today.

At home, my daughter was no problem. She was very reserved and didn't deserve a mother like me to bully her and force her to put her hands down when she was walking. When my daughter was thirteen, she was diagnosed with schizophrenia. She went to hospital and, by this time, I had a social worker who visited her there. My daughter told her she was being bullied at school because the children were sticking pencils into her and refusing to play with her. I was shocked when the social worker told me this and very upset.

Within three years, my daughter was hospitalised twice. The second time, they stopped all medication and started from scratch in order to see exactly what was wrong with her. Their assessment concluded that the first diagnosis was incorrect and she was now diagnosed as autistic. I am convinced that my daughter developed mental problems because she couldn't communicate with her peers at school due to being autistic, and also because I was depressed all the time. She told the social worker that she didn't want to tell me what was happening at school because I was sad and she didn't want to make me more sad. As children always do, they protect their parents, whether or not their parents deserve their protection.

All my daughter needed was for me to show her a lot of affection, but at that time I just couldn't show her the amount she needed, although I loved her to death. When I was in Africa, it was she who had kept me alive. I was determined to survive because I knew that, if I had died, there would be no one to care for her because she wasn't the biological child of my fiancé. In contrast, I was always confident that the family would take care of my boys.

When my daughter was about fifteen, we went for counselling together, and I discovered that a mother is often unable to bond with an autistic child. My daughter never looked into my eyes and never smiled at me. Apparently, this helps the bonding process for some parents. After the counselling, I suddenly felt a strong, loving bond with my daughter, but it wasn't as strong as it was with my boys. That is the truth! I never abused her or any of my children, and I took care of them the best way I could.

Both my daughter and her brother went to same school. The school also had problems with my son, which resulted in him getting expelled from the school permanently, although he was just five-and-a-half years old.

The head teacher called my son a wild pony, because they couldn't get him to stay still. It is obvious now that he had ADHD, but again, the teachers didn't care enough to help a black child, and at that time I had never heard of ADHD so couldn't make a judgement about his behaviour. However, someone must have told me to change his diet. It might have been the teachers. They told me not to give him bread or fizzy drinks, but nothing really helped.

During the lessons, he ran around the class without his shoes. Sometimes, he disappeared underneath the table. A gentle giant at five years old, he was the tallest among his age group and the strongest too. He played rough, but he really meant no harm. My son was too young to know his own strength.

The head teacher sarcastically suggested that she would put him in the nursery because of his immature behaviour, but then pretended to reflect on the fact that he was taller than the under-fives and would hurt them. She was just being sarcastic. She knew she had no intention of putting him in the nursery because of his age.

One day, my son's teacher's husband sadly died and she returned to work because she didn't want to stay at home alone. However, my son just carried on being himself. He was just a child. The head teacher asked me to let him stay at home and I agreed because, to be honest, although his behaviour was no different at home, sometimes I didn't take him to school because the negative news about his behaviour was often too much for me to bear alone, and I just didn't know what to do.

As a single mother, I needed family love and support as well as an education system that cared for a black child. But I had neither of these, and I just couldn't raise my children alone, due to my own childhood issues and the lack of support I had. I felt vulnerable because of depression. I was having problems with memory and expressing myself. When dealing with my son, the head teacher behaved as though she was dealing with a monkey in a zoo; there was no empathy. She was as cold as the English winter and as distant as if we were a different species.

One day, I went to the school to talk to the head teacher about the problems my children were experiencing. All three of my children were in the room. As we talked, both the had teacher and another lady were looking at my children with pure contempt and fear, as though my children were possessed. I was spoken to in a condescending way, sometimes with wicked smirks on their racist faces. My baby was on the floor in the playing area and he started crying, so I went over to comfort him and stop him from crying. That same day, social services came to our house because the school had reported to them that I had slapped my son across his face. However, when social services came, there was no swelling or marks on his face to prove such a malicious accusation. If I had slapped him as hard as they said, my son, being light-skinned with sensitive skin, would have had at least a red and swollen face.

The second incident was the final blow and after it, I wanted to return to live in London, which is where I was living before I went to Africa. One day, when my mother took my five-year-old to school, the head teacher, with no warning, met her at the entrance and refused to let my son in. The headteacher claimed that she had tried everything, but nothing was working. However, my son, being a presumptuous and confident little five-year-old, walked straight past her and off to his classroom.

Since that day, my son was never allowed into the school again. Looking back, this should not have happened. It was unprofessional. I asked myself whether the headteacher would have reacted in the same way if my son was a white child. And so, because my son now had to stay at home, social services and a child psychologist became involved with the family.

The only reason they allowed my daughter to stay at school was because she was no trouble to anyone. She was always in a world of her own and other children bullied her, whereas my son was the opposite. Though he meant no harm, he played rough with the other children and was disruptive in the classroom throughout the day.

Though it wasn't on a regular basis, the social services arranged for a teacher to teach my son at home for a year. Thereafter, he went to a small school for children up to seven years old, but he wasn't allowed to stay for dinner, which was the time when he was most hyperactive.

One day, I received a letter from my child's dad telling me that he had got married. He married the same girl I had always thought was his cousin. When I came back to England from Africa, to stop my mother from worrying, I told her that he had promised to join me in England. But this letter confirmed that he had just wanted me to leave Africa, although I had really known this deep within me at the time. That was why I told him that I would pray for him when I return home, so God could help me find a good wife to take care of him and his children. After reading the letter, my mum fainted from shock. She knew it was going to be very difficult for me in the future and she was right; boy, was she right!

Once she had recovered from fainting, she started to suffer from mini strokes and became epileptic, although, prior to reading that letter, she was well and had never had epilepsy before. It is also a possibility that her health may have deteriorated while I was in Africa, when she didn't hear from me for over six months. So now I was also caring for mum and I continued to do so until her death in 2008.

During this time, I worked part-time in a hotel as a dishwasher but I hated it. I left that job and went to work in a care home. I hated this job, too. For me, it was not enough just to work for a living. I wanted a job that was creative, fulfilling and could take me places as a high earner My shift was from 8 p.m. to 9 a.m. the next morning. There were only two of us doing nights, myself and an African male nurse. In the morning, handover took about half an hour. After we had made breakfast for the residents, we had tea with the day staff until our shift was over.

One morning, while I was making breakfast, a white female staff member came into the kitchen and, as she walked past me, she suddenly pulled my hair and quickly walked off, asking if it was my real hair. She pulled it so hard, I immediately felt tension in my forehead. As I wrote in the first chapter, when I was arguing with my fiancé, I may not be a talker, but I can roar like a lion if someone upsets me. I told her off in such a way that she started shaking.

From that moment, there was no eye contact between us. One day, I heard that she had handed in her notice and her excuse was that I had shouted at her. Following this, all the staff gave me the silent treatment. I remember saying to one of the older ladies that I was young enough to be her daughter. Her reaction was pure disgust. She said with utter scorn, "you could never be my daughter". Soon after, I received a letter stating that my employment with the care home had ended.

I had a wonderful friendship with the African male nurse. I spent most of the time talking to him about all the past and present problems in my life. He was empathetic and caring and a superb listener. He gave me lots of wise advice. I found myself going to work to talk to him; after all, I was hardly earning enough money to make a difference in my life and I hated the job. My teachers once told me that I would make a good nurse, but I knew I wouldn't. I was caring, but I was no nurse.

As soon as I got the letter, I called the African nurse and told him what had happened. He had a second job in a care home and he helped me get a job there as well. One day, we were talking with the door closed. The day staff came on shift and thought we were making out in the room because the door was closed, so they immediately phoned the manager. Apparently, they had knocked on the door, but we hadn't heard it. The next day, I received a letter telling me that my job was terminated.

Eventually, I enrolled on a government vocational course to increase my chances of securing a more fulfilling job. I also received financial help for childcare, so both my sons could stay with a childminder for a couple of hours after school and nursery.

Sadly, my studies at the college were short-lived. The childminder who was caring for my eldest son was pregnant and couldn't cope with him. She said he was a 'handful'. So, I had to leave the course and stay at home.

Now, I had to think of another plan to help my family. The thought came to me that perhaps my son would do better in a more multicultural community and so I decided that the best thing to do would be to make an effort to return to London.

Once again, my soul-friend was about to help me move towards my destiny. I got in touch with her and told her about my intention to move back to London. Fortunately for me, she had an acquaintance who was the landlord of a six-bedroom house and when she told him about me, he was happy to rent it to us. I was so determined to go that I enrolled on a keep-fit instructor course in London to remind myself that the move must take place – and it did.

London, 1992

When I moved back London, I tried to do the keep-fit course but had problems with co-ordination. We had not even begun the written work yet, which I knew I would also have struggled with. I was so embarrassed, I left the course.

We didn't stay for very long in the six-bedroom rented house because we had problems with the landlord. While I was living there, I had a dream that I was standing on a colossal wall that only a giant could attempt to stand on. In the dream, I confidently stood on the edge of the wall and jumped off, landing on the ground triumphantly. I went to WHSmith and looked this dream up in a book. It said that I would overcome every obstacle put before me. So far, I have!

Eventually, we moved into a Housing Association property that had just been built, but it was like living in a graveyard that had been cursed. There were many arguments between the neighbours. One day, a police van came with dogs and took two families away who were our immediate neighbours. When we first moved in, I was very close to my neighbour, before we, too, became enemies. We were arguing when the removal van came to move us to another property where we experienced perfect peace, but there is always calm before a storm. It wasn't very long before trouble crept into our lives again and this time the target was my eldest son.

However, before we left, I went to the library to find books on self-love. I realised that this was the only way forward, although I had a long way to go to like myself – let alone love myself (even though I didn't realise this at the time). Nevertheless the very thought of wanting to love myself was at least sending positive signals to the Universe for a change. It was also building a strong foundation upon which I could develop my confidence and become the woman I was born to be, before society had started to shape and mould me to fail in life.

I found a book with affirmations, which I wrote down and placed on both sides of my bedroom door. I affirmed these sayings out loud when I came out of my room and read them again on the back of the door before going down the stairs.

One of the exercises told me to look in the mirror and tell the person looking at me that I loved them, but I had no feelings for that person I was looking at. So, I went back to when I was a child, when the only time I had experienced pain was when my father used to beat me and my mother had left me at school for the first time. I imagined that little girl looking into a crystal ball and seeing her future and being terrified of seeing all the pain and heartache that she would one day go through, and suddenly I felt something for that little girl, and then the adult, me. It was sympathy. At last, I had some feelings for myself. I remember putting my arms around me and saying, "I like you". Every day, I told myself this until, finally, I looked into the mirror and said, "I love you". I knew I didn't mean it, but the book said I should keep on saying it until I believed it.

The book also said that I should give myself a gift. The only thing I wanted, other than a husband – a father for my children – was to read and write properly and go on to further education. I was now thirty-two years old, and I remembered the promise I made to myself in Africa, that if God helped me to return home, I would make my brain work, if it killed me.

The years were going by, as they do, and I was still depressed. It took me years to get over my experience in Africa, and also my childhood. My two eldest children were still going through their problems, and this made me so sad and frustrated that I drowned my sorrows in studying. Every year, I had to be in a learning environment, which was a learning strategy in itself. This was the reason I did so many courses; just so I could be there and listen, even though sometimes I would fall asleep because I couldn't understand the lectures. I convinced myself that I was subconsciously taking in information, even if I didn't remember or understand what I was hearing. I think my strategy worked.

College was a place I could socialise and make friends. Apart from college, I never went out. I was always at home with my children and mum. While mum stayed at home with the children, I went to evening classes to do acting, singing and guitar lessons. I also studied Japanese, Spanish and French because I had to learn basic English in order to learn other languages. I met my best friend in the Spanish class and we are still friends today. Nearly thirty years later, through DNA testing, we recently discovered that we are cousins.

I also went to college when my children were at school, but some lessons took place after school hours. The two eldest children would come home from school on their own, while my mother helped me with the youngest child until he was old enough to come home from school on his own, too.

All the courses I enrolled on were just to study English from a different angle and build confidence. Now I was ready to study basic English and Maths and other courses. The following year, I enrolled in a Pre-Access to Law course, which also covered basic English and Maths as well as general knowledge. For me, this course was ideal because I had missed out on a mainstream education. The Pre-Access course taught me about the history of English and modern law, the industrial revolution in Britain and other studies. I was learning unfamiliar words and phrases as well as basic communication skills, and feeling more confident all the time. Though I didn't pass the course, I learnt so much from them and my reading and writing skills had improved as a result of doing them.

One academic year, I studied GCSE English and passed. This was my first academic certificate. If only I could have jumped over the moon and the stars when I passed my GCSE, I would have done so. I was so happy and proud of myself. Though it was only a grade 'C', it was better than an 'E'. This paved the way for my 'studying career', which I later became obsessed with. I actually felt intelligent. The GCSE teacher told me that given where I had started from, she had never seen any student achieve so much within such a short space of time. By now, I was in my mid-30s.

The following year, I studied for an A-level in Performing Arts because I had wanted to be an actress since childhood. It was impossible for me to watch a film without pretending that I was a part of it. I did the same when I watched Junior Show Time on television in the late '60s. I remember seeing a little black boy in that show, and I used to wonder how did he had made it onto the programme? I was taught to write monologues, songs and a script to perform. I passed with a grade 'D' grade, but at least it was an A-level.

As I write this book, I am a qualified Dyslexia Tutor working as a Study Skills Teacher with both undergraduates and graduate students. Unfortunately, I am now in my early '60s. Though I feel blessed to be alive, I say unfortunately, because I should have been at this stage of my career in my 20s or even in my early 30s, so I could have provided a better life for my children. However, owing to my subnormal education, in my 20s, I couldn't read or write properly, so in my 30s, I had to study basic English and Maths instead of working and earning money to go on holidays with my children. Money doesn't buy happiness, but it sure helps.

I was a mother who couldn't help her children with their schoolwork. I couldn't even communicate effectively with the teachers, who were often condescending. As for work, I got my first job as a Dyslexia Tutor when I was 52, but by this time, my two eldest children had developed mental illness and my youngest was in prison.

During the seven stages of the human life circle in the prenatal stage, for example, we might not make it through the birth channel if we do not develop at the right time. As the saying goes, 'there is a time for everything'.

Key stage 1 is for children aged between 5 and 7 and key stage 2 is for those aged between 7 and 11. The compulsory national curriculum subjects for these stages are: English, maths, science, design and technology, history, geography and art and design, starting at the basic level according to the child's age. At a special school in the '60s, there was no curriculum and children never progressed beyond the very basics.

Although I achieved my academic goals in later life, I did so at my children's expense. While I was studying, we lived in poverty so I could focus on my studies. You may ask why couldn't I work *and* study? After all, I teach dyslexic students who are working full-time, studying full-time and trying to raise their children. However, because I was dyslexic and made educationally subnormal, I needed more time to study, so I couldn't work while studying at the same time.

Looking back, I put my learning before my children. I remember saying to myself that I would learn, even if it killed me. I said this several times, and I meant it. I noticed that if I chewed chewing gum and ate it, it kept me awake and helped me concentrate. I was getting fatter and fatter every day, but I didn't care; I was learning. However, in my '30s, I ended up with very high cholesterol because of my 'study diet' and the stress of being a single mother with children who needed a lot of attention. So, when I said I would study even if it kills me, my death wish almost came to pass. Most of the time, I didn't remember what I had learnt, but at least my comprehension and understanding were getting better and the words didn't get in a tangle with each other when I was reading.

It was more important to me to have an 'academic career' than to study for a career where I could work and take care of my children and the home. I honestly didn't know what else to do. Apart from a desire to be in the entertainment industry, there was no job that I was good at. I tried doing care work, but it made me depressed. The only activity that made me happy was studying. I couldn't commit to a full-time job, because I needed that time to study. If I wasn't at college, I often spent the whole day in the library, remembering nothing when I left. Some courses were from 10 a.m. to 3 p.m. As the children got older, I went to college from 9 a.m. I remember my mother telling me to stay at home with my children instead of going to college or going to work. But I thought it was mean of her to say such a thing, because I was thinking of the future, not the present. I was also trying to survive the best way I could mentally.

While I was living out my dream of educating myself, my two eldest children continued to have problems at school with both learning and interacting with other children. I realised it didn't help the situation by moving my son from a small city to London, with its larger multiracial communities. Though the head teacher was black at the first school he went to, this didn't help with my son's problems. Also, there were a few black teachers in London, but this didn't make a difference either, although they were more patient, empathic and caring than their white counterparts.

Sadly, history began to repeat itself again. My daughter was never disruptive in the classroom; she was only quiet. At the new school, the children began bullying her for no reason, other than for being reserved and unable to communicate like them. My son became distressed when he saw his sister being bullied and tried to help, but he only got into trouble as a result.

Unlike a white headteacher, the black headteacher was more empathetic and patient with both my son and me. Sometimes, he disrupted the class because he couldn't keep still or pay attention. When his teacher sent him to the headteacher, she spent time talking to him and giving him one-to-one support in her office. Besides this, she made an effort to get to know me, to find out how she could best help the family, whereas the white teachers were cold. I tried to attend as many meetings as possible and also parent evenings, but there were never any constructive solutions to help my children remain in a mainstream school.

My daughter never went to a special school but sadly, like me, my son went to one. At that time, I didn't realise the negative impact this type of school was having on my life, therefore I didn't know I needed to fight to stop my child from going to a special school. They could have met my children's needs at the school if they had one-to-one support in the classroom. I am not sure why the headmistress didn't arrange this for them; perhaps she was restricted with what she could do?

It wasn't until my son went to an SEN school that they gave him extra support. The support worker was a black male, who was not only like a role model to my son, but also a father figure. My son said he really helped him. Besides this, unlike in the '60s, he was fortunate to go to an SEN school that had a school curriculum, so he could take exams and pass them. He also did work experience and received excellent feedback from the staff. My argument is, why couldn't he have had the same support in a mainstream school? I would have preferred it if he had remained in a mainstream school and not gone to a special school as I'd done. This was a trend predicted by Bernard

Coard, when children end up trapped in the system like their parents because of systemic racism in the school system.

When my daughter was thirteen years old,, she disappeared for an entire day during the school holidays. I was about to call the police when she came home. For this reason, when I broke up from college, I stayed at my mum's house because her door could be locked from the inside so my daughter couldn't get out.

While we were staying at my mother's place, my daughter stayed in the room the whole time and was talking to herself even more than ever. She was having delusions that she was the Queen of England and hallucinating that she had a rat under her arm. My eldest son was now ten years old, and he was just as hyperactive as he was when he was five, while my seven-year-old son was a quiet child, well behaved both at home and at school. I really believe he was absorbing all that was going on in the family home, and what he was experiencing had a negative impact on him. He may have been depressed at not having a voice to express what he was going through. I now feel that his needs were neglected because if I wasn't studying, I had to attend to the needs of my eldest children. At sixteen years old, his voice became apparent and all hell broke loose. Serves me right for neglecting him all those years.

As for my mother, her epilepsy returned and throughout the day she was having fits and couldn't remember anything afterwards, not even her own name. I was very depressed and stressed while trying to do my 'A'-level homework and look after my eldest two children and my mother at the same time. My heart was so very broken. I was lonely and confused about what was happening to the only family I had wanted since I was a child.

One day, it was nearly bedtime and it had been a really long and very stressful day. I was trying to write a monologue to perform when I returned to college which would count towards my exams. The plan was to end the day putting extensions in my hair when everyone was sleeping. Doing my hair was therapeutic, so it was my way to relax after a very stressful day. My mother and daughter had already gone to bed and I was trying to get the boys to settled in for the night.

I went into the bathroom to do my hair. Suddenly I heard my youngest son screaming. As I said, it had been a long day, and I just wanted to spend some time pampering myself. When I heard the noise, I just flipped. I marched angrily to the room, opened the door and threw the blow-dryer towards the bed where my two sons were just playing instead of sleeping. I was fully aware that they wouldn't get hurt because they were both fighting under the duvet. But then my youngest suddenly popped his head out from the duvet and the blow-dryer hit him in his forehead. The blow to his head happened so quickly, he didn't realise what had happened at first. I rushed him downstairs to clean him up and it was at that point that I realised how serious his injury was. I panicked when I saw the bone under his skin. I was so shocked and he was worried about me. When he saw the expression as I gently held his little face with my two hands, he said, "mummy, don't worry, it's not hurting". But his forehead had opened up and I could see the bone. I was shocked and disgusted with myself. I couldn't even cry; I froze. I was thinking that he would be scarred for life. I said out loud, "look what I have done to my beautiful son". I was so sorry and remorseful. I quickly pulled myself together and called a taxi to take us to the hospital, which wasn't far away from my mother's place.

When we arrived, we didn't have to wait long to be seen because he was just seven years old. An exquisite doctor came out to attend to him. I remember thinking that because she was so beautiful, she could imagine being scarred herself and would do a perfect job on a beautiful child, which she did.

Things got even worse after that terrible incident, which laid the foundation for more troubles. It was like a chain reaction of bad omens and they kept coming and coming. Thereafter, inevitably, social services got involved.

The next day, social services came with male and female police officers. They asked my children a lot of questions. My youngest said that I had deliberately hit him, and continued to believe this until adulthood; he never forgave me. I guess it must have looked like that to him. To him, it must have been like a sudden blow to his head, not realising that I was nowhere near him. I was at the door when I threw the blow-dryer as they were both playing under the duvet, so I clearly hadn't mean to hurt him.

As for my daughter, I took her to the doctor several times, but was told repeatedly that nothing was wrong with her. When I was at mum's house, I called social services about my daughter because I didn't want her to wander off again. She was also acting strangely and it was getting worse. I didn't know what would happen when I left mum's place to go back home after the school holidays. I couldn't leave her in the house alone, or leave her with mum. And as selfish as this may sound to some of my readers, I had to get back to college or

I would have gone crazy, even though, when I was at college, there was often conflict between me and the students because my energy was so negative and I was so emotional, due to what was happening at home. I was also worried about my mother's health.

I called social services for the last time, determined not to hang up without getting them to listen to me. The first time they had come to the house was because I had accidentally hit my son and they just dealt with that particular situation in order to protect him. That same year, he was placed on the protective register for children.

This time when I rang them, I was determined that they should return to the house to help me. With great emphasis and concern, I explained the whole situation about my family to them. I told them that I couldn't cope with my daughter because something was wrong with her and I didn't know what it was. They just told me to get on with my responsibilities as a mother. I then told them that if they didn't come for her, I would put her on the street. I didn't mean this, but that's how desperate I was for them to help me.

Eventually, about three or four hours later, social services came, and they didn't look happy to see me; their attitude towards me was the same as it had been on the phone. As a mother, I already felt guilty, but they made me feel worse. That night, they took my daughter and placed her with a foster parent. Though I was relieved, I was also very sad that I had failed her, but I didn't know what else to do. The foster parent was a psychiatric nurse, who recognised her symptoms as being like schizophrenia, both in her behaviour and in her writing. My daughter was always reading books and writing about many things, including her feelings.

The foster parent then called the doctor to assess her, while the ambulance and police waited outside, as they did in those days. Thereafter, they admitted her into the adolescent unit at a mental hospital. She was just thirteen years old.

They were keen to diagnose my daughter with schizophrenia at just thirteen years old. It wasn't until she was eighteen years old, when she went to hospital again, that they discovered she was autistic. However, by this time, she had become addicted to psychosis medication for many years, but now she refuses to take any medication as an adult.

Going back to when I daughter was a young teenager, the neighbours thought we were a weird family, especially when my daughter was becoming unwell and would hide in the bushes instead of going to school. We lived in a cul-de-sac. When you entered the street, it felt as though the houses were built on an ancient graveyard, because there were so many arguments between all the neighbours. The police were always there and one day, a police van came with dogs and took two neighbours away because they were fighting. Another two neighbours, who lived next door to each other, often called the police on each other more or less at the same time.

Though my neighbour and I were friends, we didn't get on sometimes over our children. My son was very hyperactive and played roughly with her children, but he didn't know his own strength; he meant no harm. He was a little gentle giant; however, my neighbour showed no empathy towards him. One particular neighbour told her children to throw stones at my son, if he played rough with them and they got hurt. They also didn't like my mother because she was always defending her grandchildren and chasing the next-door neighbour's cat from our house.

Before my daughter was admitted to hospital, I got a temporary part-time job in a factory and saved up to send my children on holiday in Europe with their paternal auntie. The bullying was so bad in our neighbourhood and at their schools that they desperately needed a break. At this stage, none of the neighbours were talking to me. There was no family support, and I felt isolated from the world. Though I continued to study, I was heavily burdened with pure stress, which resulted in me being diagnosed with high cholesterol, despite being only in my 30s.

While my family was on holiday, I stayed at home to reflect on everything that was going on. I desperately needed to be on my own, just to relax. I also did a deep spring clean and decorated. When they returned home, the house was fresh and clean, but it wasn't long before it was a tip again. It was after that trip that my daughter became seriously unwell and was admitted to hospital for the first time.

The tension with my neighbours was so bad that I asked the council to move us and, with the help of my social worker, we were moved. On the day we were going to leave, I was arguing with one of my neighbours when a big removal van came and took us away forever. My neighbour across the road came over to apologise and gave me a hug, and all was forgiven.

Unlike my daughter, for the first time, the two boys went into foster care while I moved into the new house to prepare for their return. They met foster children they kept in touch with for a long time. They saw themselves as siblings and cared for each other like they would in their biological family, but they took pleasure in calling themselves 'foster sisters and brothers'. I wanted them to go into foster care because the foster parent could get an allowance to buy them new clothes and take them on a trip, which I couldn't afford to do. I also needed the time alone because I was depressed, stressed, and confused about the future.

We moved to a very quiet area where the neighbour's children didn't even play outside, so my children wouldn't be tempted to go out to play. Now, I had to think about how I was going to keep them occupied because they were getting older. When I was doing my Performing Arts A-level, my mother used to bring them to watch me perform. So, after moving to the new place, I thought it would be in the best interest of my eldest son to get him involved in drama and singing lessons, while the youngest went to football. They also went to private lessons to study English and maths, but eventually they had to stop, because I couldn't keep up with the payments; I was always unemployed and studying.

Our new environment was a better place for my daughter to come home to when she came back from the hospital for the second time. She was eighteen years old when she came back home to live with me. On one occasion, I arranged for us to go to a make-up pampering session. I also arranged for her to go to the seaside with the church but they complained that she wasn't interacting with the children.

While my daughter was living with me, I thought this would be an opportunity to teach her to cook, something my mother never did with me, but it was impossible to get her to do anything. One day, I was teaching her to cook chicken when suddenly she threw the chicken seasoning in my face and ran upstairs to her room. I didn't have any patience left and I gave up quite easily after that. On one occasion, she shouted at me "you're supposed to be my mother". And sadly, I shouted back at her, "yes but I'm not a nurse, and I just can't do this alone". And because I was her mother and I love my daughter, I saw the pain, frustration and disappointment in her eyes, but I just couldn't help her and nurture her the way I should have done as a mother; basically, I was a bad mother. She wanted me to be more affectionate by giving her hugs and kisses and talking to her, but I didn't do this often, not even with the boys; although they got more affection from me than my daughter. Nevertheless, the boys complained that I didn't talk to them enough as I was either studying or depressed.

One day, I had to make the most difficult decision to call the doctor for my daughter. Her mental health was deteriorating because she refused to take her medication. In those days, when you called the mental health doctor, the police and the ambulance came also. She didn't speak to me for a year while she was admitted to hospital, but I still went to visit her.

As for my eldest son, when we left the old house, things got worse for him. He was growing taller and even more handsome, but he still had low self-esteem and confidence, and often complained to me that he had problems with his thoughts. He also continued to find it difficult to fit in with his peers at school and, as a result, became a target for bullying.

HOW I FAILED MY CHILDREN
BECAUSE THE BRITISH EDUCATION SYSTEM FAILED ME

On his way home from school one day, a group of boys approached my son and one of them smashed a broken bottle into his neck; just missing the jugular vein. They were all about the same age. My son was thirteen years old and the boy was fourteen. I had to take time off college when it happened because I was so disturbed by the whole incident. We went to court and they found the boy guilty. He was sentenced to community service.

One day, my son came to me and told me something that had happened to him in Africa when he stayed overnight with the woman his dad had introduced to me as his cousin but who was, in fact, his girlfriend.

Now a teenager, he told me what took place when he was with her. He said she raped him! I replied by saying, "what do you mean?" He went on to explain that she tried to have sexual intercourse with him and when he couldn't do it properly, she became furious and hit him; he was just five years old. I froze as I tried to comprehend what my son was telling me. I was so very angry, I felt hopeless because she wasn't living down the road where I could go and confront her. I was angry and shocked, while some part of me wanted to disbelieve what he was saying. Apparently, she and her brothers had come to the hotel where we were staying and performed a ritual (voodoo) by bowing down to my son. Because he was my ex-finance's first child, the ritual would be so effective, it would make his father marry her. Lucky for her the ritual worked, because after we left Africa, they got married and had two boys; although they got divorced in the end. But what she did to my child really affected him because he truly believes that she took his soul, which has had a great impact on his mental health.

If a grown woman tries to force a five-year-old child to have sex with her and then punishes him when he doesn't perform like a man, this is bound to have an effect on the child, both mentally and physically, as well as his ability to have intimate relationships.

Although is was just five years old, my son said he never felt the same when he came back from Africa, and later blamed me for taking him there. I didn't know what to do with this information and how to help him. In retrospect, I often wonder why I never thought of taking him to the doctor to see if they could offer him counselling. At this time, I was at university, and maybe I was too busy writing essays to take him to the doctor. Instead, I called my ex-fiancé's family in Europe and told them what my son had told me. They told me they had accused the woman of doing the same thing to his other children, and they also said they didn't know of his whereabouts.

It shocked me when I discovered that my daughter had written to him because I had written to him on numerous occasions and sent pictures and I didn't hear back from him. It was through my daughter that he made contact with the family again; by now she was twenty one years old and her brother was eighteen I told him what his girlfriend had done to our son while we were in Africa, but he didn't believe me.

My son really believes that his dad's girlfriend took his soul and for this reason he is trapped in his body. He is aware that it is maybe possible that he could have developed mental health problems but not to the extent that he couldn't live a normal life, for example work, marry and have children. I have tried to reassure him that it is impossible for someone to take your soul because your soul belongs to God.

It is a spirit like God, with no shape or form, therefore no one can hold it or touch it; it is like the wind.

I am convinced that my children's experiences in Africa, together with my inability to provide or care for them financially on our return to England, also had a devastating effect on their mental health because I continued living on benefits and studying, instead of working. The obsession to learn was still my priority. I honestly didn't know what job I could do apart from cleaning, and I didn't want to do that for the rest of my life. My mother had always helped me to buy clothes for my youngest, but the eldest two were my responsibility and I did my best; I did without so they could have. They had more clothes than I did and their rooms always had the best furniture and carpet. My children used to dress much better than I did, yet my eldest son thought he looked poorer than his peers and it worried him tremendously.

When I started university and received my student grant, I gave my eldest son money to buy clothes. He needed clothes to go for job interviews. On his way home, a group of boys who used to be his friends beat him up and took the clothes he'd bought. They even took the ones he was wearing, so he came home half-naked. He had already become depressed when one of his friends stabbed him just above his jugular vein when he was about fourteen years old, so it really affected his confidence and self-esteem even more when they beat him up and took his new clothes.

That year, he left school, and I went with him to college to enrol in a full-time sound engineering music course and I also took him to another college to enrol in a sound engineering evening class with a former music teacher of mine. I also encouraged my son to work part-time while he studied, so I helped him apply for a job in a restaurant, but the school wouldn't give him a reference, so he didn't get the job. A year later, he was arrested for stealing mobile phones. When I asked him why he did it, he said he wanted to buy clothes. He went to prison for three years, but he served just over a year. While he was there, he told them he was depressed, but instead of counselling him, like they would a white person, they gave him psychosis medication when they sent him to the prison hospital, and he ended up with lockjaw when they gave him the medication. It is a fact that my son's experience mirrors that of many black boys in England. They are more likely to be diagnosed with mental health problems than whites. My son was in prison for just over a year. When he came home, he was overweight, mentally disturbed, and has remained addicted to medication until this very day. He is nearly thirty-nine years old. As I write these words, my eyes are filling up with tears because he is in hospital.

Distressed about the entire ordeal of my son going to prison, I couldn't write my dissertation, so I asked for an extension because I had to support my son during the court case and visit him in prison. I also had to be there for my daughter, who was living with foster parents, and my elderly mother, who was in her eighties and living with me.

As always, I was thinking about the future. I didn't want my son to come out of prison to live in the same area where those boys lived, so I wrote to Tony Blair. I told him about my life and what had happened to my son and why I wanted to move to a quiet area. I wanted to move so that when my son came out of prison, he could go outside without worrying that he might see his bullies.

One day, my landlord rang me to say he had received a letter from 10 Downing Street. I wrote to the government because I wanted to move out of the area. As a result, not only did my landlord place me on the waiting list to move, but he also placed me at the top of the list. Within months of receiving my letter, I was offered a beautiful, four-bedroom house in a very quiet area in a distant borough. So, when my son came home, he could take long walks without worrying that he might see any of the boys who used to bully him.

By this time, my daughter was living in an independent care home and had a caring support worker; she was doing very well, and I visited her as often as I could. Sometimes, we went out for dinner, or we went for a long walk, although she was always reluctant for us to go for walks together because she worried that my feet would hurt when I walked for a long distance.

Until now, I have only mentioned my youngest child briefly. He was busy growing up and trying to understand the environment he was born into, which was often filled with hysteria. This is my opinion; he might disagree, if he gets the chance to read this one day, which I hope he will. Like his sister and brother, he was a very pleasant little boy, but unlike them, he could play on his own and also play and interact with other children. He wasn't hyperactive and labelled as being disruptive in the classroom like his brother. You can only imagine what he was going through to see his siblings struggling with so many diversities, and to have a mother who was very sad.

When my daughter was sent to a mental health hospital, it really confused me and made me even more depressed. I had to attend conference meetings consisting of doctors and other professionals who were caring for my daughter. At these meetings, like the TV programme This is Your Life, they put my life before me on the table in a report written by people who were judging us according to a book. Sometimes, after the meetings, I became too disturbed by what we talked about even to go to college, and I felt the same way by the time I went to university because I was still going to these meetings, not just for my daughter, but also for my eldest son and for my elderly mother. I was so preoccupied with either my other two children, my mother or studying that I was unable to think about how the environment at home was affecting my youngest child, who didn't seem to have any obvious problems. He was only seven years old when his sister was admitted into a mental health hospital and fourteen when his brother went to prison.

By the time my eldest son went to hospital, his little brother was at the age where he could refuse to accompany me when visiting him. He went to visit him on his own terms, whenever he wanted, but he never went to see his sister. When he was a very young child, he was very quiet and too young to express his worries as children normally do. I don't know when he started taking drugs but I later discovered, quite by chance, that he was taking drugs when he was a teenager. My partner's daughter came to stay with us for a short while and said she couldn't stay with us because my son was taking drugs. I was a naïve mother and I was just too busy with everything else to see the signs, although I wouldn't have known what the signs were. And because he was so quiet when he was little, and caused no trouble, I didn't worry about him, which I should have done.

A mother's instinct is always right. When he was about six years old, because of my two eldest children's problems and because of my depression, I had a strong feeling that the environment I was bringing him up in would affect him. We were isolated from a family I wasn't close to, anyway. And I had no real friends; not even one I could call my bosom friend. This could have been because I had moved from England to Africa, then from one [county] to another and from one borough to another. Though I didn't realise it at the time, everywhere I went I carried with me a negative aura, not just because of my past experiences, but also because of what I was going through as a single mother, so it was difficult to make and keep friends. Moving from one place to another must have affected my children, too.

I contacted my first cousin, who lived in another [county] and whose lifestyle I had always admired, to ask if he could raise my youngest child for a few years. He had a quiet disposition and lived a decent life with his wife and a little girl. He turned me down. I later discovered that he was angry that I had asked him in the first place.

As much as it broke my heart, I then took my eldest son to live in Europe with his uncle and his wife. He was nine years old at the time. They were childless, although they did have children later on. They lived in a block of flats and somehow my son managed to turn off the lights in the entire building. He also rode a friend's bicycle down a steep hill, fell off and broke his collarbone. As a result, he ended up in hospital, so I rushed to be by his side.

My son had a gentle nature and was very playful. All the children in the building wanted to play with him; I think it was because he was the only black child around, but his uncle's wife just couldn't cope with all the attention and his hyperactive behaviour. She was also trying to have a baby and found my son's behaviour very stressful. She told me she had many brothers and sisters, but had never come across anyone like my son. So, I brought him back home to grow up with his siblings, come what may.

As for my youngest, he had always had a quiet disposition; perhaps that is why I wanted him to live with my cousin for a while, who had a same nature. However, despite being a well-behaved child at home, when he went to secondary school, he was reluctant to do his schoolwork. When I attended a parents' evening, his teachers and I were confused because he was so bright; he was in the highest class at school. I then got him into a sports school because he was good at both football and basketball. When he was older, he taught the younger children football, and he was featured in the school's prospectus for that.

One day, the school called me. They were very concerned that he wasn't doing his work in the class. At this time, his older brother was doing very well at school, although by now he was going to an ESN school and later went to prison. As well as not doing classwork, my youngest son never brought home homework.

I am not sure if he was taking drugs at this time, which would explain his behaviour. Despite all this, he got on very well with his peers and he was never bullied at school; he even had a best friend. However, he did get picked on when he was out with his friends.

My son stood out because he was very tall, outspoken and handsome. He was constantly being 'rushed', as it was called back then. The first time it happened, his collarbone was dislocated. Thereafter, it popped out every time he was 'rushed' or when he moved swiftly. Then he would have to go to hospital to have the collarbone popped back in. They had to sedate him in order to do this and gave him a morphine injection for the pain. This happened every time he was attacked and beaten up. The constant 'rushing' made him paranoid about going outside for a while. Although he got over this eventually, I don't think he ever fully regained his confidence.

When he turned sixteen, he showed no signs of wanting to work or even to go to college. His best friend came to his borough to go to college, thinking my son would join him, but he never did. My son said to me, "I have never seen you work, and I don't want to give you money". I told him not to waste time watching me, but to spend that time in making his life much better than mine. I told him that "education is a passport around the world" because with an excellent education he could get a job at home or abroad. If I was educated, or had a career, I could have worked when I went to Africa and possibly I would not have returned to England. I realised this when I was in Africa and that is why I promised myself that when I return to England, I would go to college. But, he never listened to me. He was so unlike his big brother, who allowed me to take him to college to enrol on a course.

Nevertheless, this didn't stop me from writing his CV and sending it to nearly every hotel both in and outside our area. I also handed it in person to nearby shops, stores, shopping centres and restaurants, including Caribbean takeaway shops. The only reply we received was from McDonald's, who offered him an interview. I spoke with the manager, and she was very keen to meet him. But again, he refused to go for the interview.

Two years went by and he still wasn't working or going to college. Looking back, I think he may have been depressed. Why not? Throughout his young days, I had been depressed and his siblings had developed mental health problems. Also, he never got over losing his hair when his brother took him to a barber and he caught ringworm, which resulted in alopecia.

Sometimes, if my son didn't go out, he would stay in his bedroom all day until it was time to eat. I often called him down to the living room to talk to me, but he refused to come. My father never spoke and mother and my teachers hardly spoke to me so I hardly spoke to anyone, even my children. Also, I was very depressed so absorbed myself in studying. I didn't work so I didn't have money to take my children on holidays. Therefore, it is understandable that my little son refused to speak to me.

When my children were little, it was easier to speak with my eldest son because he was very observant and caring. He often asked me, "why are you depressed, mum?". He used to write a note of encouragement and put it under my door because he wanted to cheer me up. Later in life, he often blamed me for his own depression because I made him sad when I was sad. He was right about this and I take full responsibility for the part I played in making my children dysfunctional.

The years were going by and I often reminded my youngest son that he was getting older and should either go to college or seek employment. When he was eighteen, he still wasn't working and was becoming more and more aggressive, disrespectful and overtly rude to me.

Around this time, at last, I was in a relationship. Though I had had relationships before, they didn't work out. We met in the lift when I was on my way to university to attend an introduction day to an MA in Professional Writing. I thought this man was a potential partner, who would one day become my husband. He was very dark-skinned, handsome with very big eyes, smartly dressed and seemed to have very good manners.

We started living together when my son was nineteen and still showing no signs of doing anything proactive to prepare himself for a successful and prosperous future. He had no dreams or desires to do anything at all, no matter how unrealistic those dreams or desires might be; if he did, he never spoke to me about them. One day, I asked him what he wanted to do and after observing him, I advised him to study psychology. He agreed and I paid for him to do a home study course, but nothing came of it.

My partner and my youngest son didn't get on. My partner couldn't understand why my son wasn't doing anything with his life, and he wasn't prepared to embrace him, despite the fact that my son didn't have a father or even an uncle as a role model in his life. As a matter of fact, it turned out that this man wasn't in love with me from the start, so how could he love and embrace my children as his own?

I remember a bitter argument between the two of them when my son yelled out in a sad and disappointed voice, "you have brought no love into this house". He was right about that. From the moment this man moved in, the atmosphere became toxic. But I was in denial and turned a blind eye to what was happening in our relationship. I tried to work on the relationship, despite the man being a narcissist and extremely critical of everyone else except himself. He thought he was perfect. He saw my children as inferior to his children and he detested my youngest; yet I still stayed with him.

He lived with us for nearly six years, and though there were some good times between us, as is always the case in every relationship or situation, the atmosphere in my home became more and more toxic – as it had in my father's house. Heated arguments often resulted in the police coming to the house. Once, we had an argument and my neighbour called the police and he told them it was my fault. He was a violent man, but he knew that if he abused me physically, I wouldn't have allowed it and he would have had to leave.

During arguments between my partner and my son, I would always be in the middle to protect my son. No matter how hard he tried, he could never get near him to hurt him, and no matter how hard he tried to move me out of the way, he couldn't. He mentioned once, in bed, that he couldn't understand how I fixed my body firmly on the ground so he couldn't move me, although he knew he was stronger than I was. I simply told him I am a mother.

When I stood in front of my partner when he was arguing with my son, my son must have thought I wasn't on his side and that I was protecting my partner. He didn't realise that I was always protecting him. I wouldn't have allowed anyone to hurt him in my presence, not even his own father, if he had been around.

Nevertheless, although I knew I couldn't trust my partner with my son, I still wanted my relationship to work. It had taken me sixteen years to meet someone who I really loved. Although I knew he didn't love me, I believed he would have grown to love me. This relationship lasted for nearly six years because I didn't love myself.

When he left and got married a few months later, my son became even more resentful towards me; I presume because he thought I had always put my ex-partner before him. But I hadn't. By now, my son had become even more verbally and physically abusive towards me, perhaps because I didn't have anyone in the house to protect me. I was now single and my dear mother had passed away the year before, so I was still in mourning and so was my son, because they had been very close. He was now twenty-two and still wasn't working or going to college.

Before my mother died, I had a sudden urge to visit my father's graveside. It took me nearly five hours by coach to travel to my home town. When I came back home, my mother was in the hospice and my eldest son was in hospital, so I couldn't decide who to visit first. I went home instead. The next day, I received a call from the hospice to say that my mother was unresponsive but still breathing. I panicked and in despair I ordered the hospice to rush her to the hospital, saying that I would meet her there. The ambulance and I arrived at the hospital at the same time.

I called my daughter, my youngest son and my soul-friend and her daughter and they all met me at the hospital. We were all at her bedside when she took her last breath at 3:33 p.m. My youngest son made a note of the time she died because I wasn't aware of it.

After I had laid my mother to rest, I had a dream that I was giving birth, and I knew it was my mother's soul returning through me. Oh, how much I miss her still, and how profoundly sad I am that I couldn't make her happy in her last years.

My daughter wrote a beautiful tribute to her grandmother. Her brothers weren't at her funeral, but my youngest paid his last respects to her, as her body lay peacefully overnight in the living-room before her burial. When my partner came home from work, he bowed to her before going to the bedroom. I had to be strong at the funeral and I tried not to cry; even when my mother's body was lowered down into the ground. I was afraid my emotions would get the better of me, which would cause me to stutter when I had to make a speech about her life; I wanted to make my mother proud, so I tried very hard to suppress my emotions. However, after the funeral, I cried every day for a very long time.

My relationship with my partner continued to deteriorate after the passing of my mother until, a year later, it finally came to an abrupt end overnight when I threw his belongings out into the garden. Five months later, he married the girlfriend he had been with while we were together. I could see that my son was relieved when this man was finally out of my life, but I wasn't sure if he was happy that he didn't have to see him again or happy that I was now alone once more. He knew how important it had always been to me to be in a relationship.

The relationship between my son and I continued to deteriorate well into his late twenties. There were no signs of him changing his behaviour and attitude to life. It was, and still is, as if he had no dreams or direction in life. If a heart could burst into a thousand pieces, mine would for my children. I live with a troubled heart every day because of them.

During this time, I had thrown my son out of the house frequently. He always came back, though, and I always opened the door to him, although sometimes I didn't. When I didn't open the door, he would break the window. One day, when he was around twenty-six years old, I called him and told him that if he didn't do something with his life, either he would have to leave or I would. Just before his thirtieth birthday, I relocated to a smaller property and, with immense sorrow, my son became homeless. Realizing that I had caused my son to become homeless meant I couldn't sleep at night and consumed alcohol so heavily that I became ill. It prompted me to change my lifestyle, or else I would have died. It was during this terrible time that I began praying differently to how I was taught to pray as a child. I used to pray in the morning and last thing at night, but because my son was homeless, I began praying whenever I ate, which was three times a day or even more because I didn't know if he was eating. I prayed to God to send the angels to protect and feed him.

Let me go back to the moment when my relationship with my partner came to an end. After my mother's death, I began preparing myself for the time when the relationship would end. One night, I was about to get into bed when, for no reason, my partner told me he would never love me. I felt a dreadful sensation which arose from my belly and shot up to my chest until I felt my head swelling. Immediately, I got off the bed, bent down on my knees and began praying in the name of Jesus. I prayed "please God, prepare me for the time when he will go, in the name of Jesus". After that night, I didn't feel right mentally. I later had a brain scan and a blood test.

The end finally came on what would have been my mother's ninety-first birthday, if she had lived. He stayed out overnight and came home in the morning. I told him that, as a result of my blood test, I might have a brain tumour, although the doctor said that my symptoms might be stress-related and I shouldn't worry. He cold heartedly replied, "It has nothing to do with me, we are finished". Although this was the news I had been expecting, it still made me very sad; I was in shock. What he said next was like rubbing my nose in the mess I had unknowingly created because of childhood trauma and not loving myself. Despite the fact that he was in a relationship with another woman, he wanted to stay with me and sleep with me in the same bed, while he saved up for a place. Immediately I thought, NO! He had wasted nearly six years of my life, and I wasn't going to allow him to waste any more. So, the next morning, I made him a cup of tea and as soon as he left, I put his belongings outside in the garden. The morning after that, I felt really guilty about what I had done and got down on my knees to ask for God's forgiveness. I promised myself I would never do that to anyone again.

A year before our relationship ended, what little respect he had for me went out of his heart when most of my family did not attend my mother's funeral. This would never have happened in his country in Africa. He actually said that it wouldn't happen anywhere on the continent of Africa.

My cousin was going to get married either that weekend or the weekend after the burial. Nevertheless, she could still have come to the funeral. Perhaps she thought I was snubbing their mother's last gift to her sister before she died, when she bought a plot for her to be buried in after her death. But I wanted my mother to be buried in the county where my children and I lived. This was the aunty who used to call me backward because I went to a backward school. The same aunty who, when I was twelve years old, allowed her son to spit in my face when I told them I had run away because her husband was sexually abusing me. She probably thought that I wouldn't be intelligent enough to work and plan a funeral. They buried their mother, so why couldn't I bury mine, too?

I felt like I'd been bullied and pushed against a wall at a crucial time in my life, when I had just lost my mother and had never planned a funeral before. So, I proved them wrong. I planned my mother's funeral and invited them to it. They didn't come. Nor did they even send a card. Despite all this, if my partner really loved me, he would not have disrespected me just because my mother's family didn't attend her funeral.

After ten years, through my ex-partner's daughter, we met again because he wanted us to rekindle our relationship, but I sent him off on his bicycle to no-man's-land, because I had finally learnt to love myself. As for my mother's family, it's their shame for turning their backs on the last chance to say goodbye to their only surviving maternal aunt.

It wasn't long after this relationship ended, that my youngest son went to prison. The first time he went, I was so shocked and distressed that I didn't have any food and water for three days. I stayed in the house, prayed earnestly to God and read psalms in the Bible. The next time he went to prison, I prayed and fasted again for three days and read the Bible; this time, I was very weak and disappointed with my son. The third time he went to prison, I prayed, but I didn't fast; I just left him in the hands of God because I could see he wasn't ready to change. I will forever pray for my children and their offspring. As I write this to you, my son has been to prison several times, and he still isn't working or studying. Yet still I have hope! Someone once said to me, "it is not the beginning, it is the end that matters" and I believe that all my children will, one day, tell their story, about how they triumphed over their adversities and won.

As a mother, I saw the potential in my children. My daughter loved animals, so I got her volunteering work on a farm nearby (hoping she might one day become a vet), while my eldest son wanted to be an actor. He was also interested in music, so I encouraged him to enrol in a sound engineering course at college and go to drama lessons; we often went to watch him perform. As for my last born, he was excellent at football and basketball, so he went to a sports school. He was so good at basketball that they even put a picture of him playing on the school's prospectus. I was hoping he would become a famous football player like his cousin, Vivian Anderson. Vivian was the first black football player to play for England on 29 November 1978, at the tender age of twenty-two.

Had I gone to a mainstream school and received both an education and support as a slow learner, as ambitious as I am, it is highly unlikely that I would have achieved my academic goals and fulfilled my desire to become an actress. I couldn't read and write properly or reason with others, so I didn't have the confidence or self-esteem to communicate effectively with people my age. Therefore, I wasn't an interesting person to be around, which made me become a loner and, for this reason, I brought up my children in isolation also, which wasn't healthy for them. In addition, I didn't know what job to do, because I was creative and a performer. I didn't want to be a packer or a cleaner, but if you can't read or write, what else can you do? In those days, if you couldn't do maths, you couldn't work in a shop. So these were the jobs I did in the early days of my life before I had children. A single mother now in her thirties, I spent my time preparing for higher education and, in my forties, I spent it studying as an undergraduate, rather than working. By the time I started to work and earn a descent wage at 52, it was too late. My children had grown up and were now institutionalised.

In truth, not every ambitious, talented actor is successful, and perhaps I wouldn't have been either. However, because of my ambitious and very determined nature, if I hadn't become a successful actress, I wouldn't have given up on my dreams. Instead, I probably would have taught Performing Arts, or become a director or a bestselling author and later in my life, I would have become a politician I would have been a happier, more confident person living my dream, been an exemplary mother and had children when the time was right to do so.

I had my children not just because I wanted a family, but also because I didn't know what else to do, so I thought I may as well become a wife and a mother. For this reason, it is difficult to accept that I ended up being a mother without a husband. I wanted my children to have the father that I had never had and a beautiful home. My plan was to study painting and decorating so I could decorate the house and make it beautiful. I would then learn to cook dishes from various parts of the world and, finally, I would learn hairdressing, so I could have a business and help my husband. But what I really wanted to do was to go to university and study to become an actress, if only I could read and had the confidence.

If my destiny hadn't been affected by racism, I would not have been depressed and penniless when I became a single mother. I would have been more financially secure and provided a better life for my children; even if they went on to develop mental illness, at least my life would have had a more positive impact on their lives and I would have been mentally stronger to take care of them.

The racist British Education System tried to change my destiny, which, in turn, affected the destiny of my children. This meant that I had to spend time recreating my destiny (at the expense of my children), instead of working towards it at the right age, when I could have achieved something and made a difference in my life for the future before becoming too old to do so.

My precious children got lost in the maze of it all. I needed more time to learn when I went on to higher education, so I couldn't work to take care of them and couldn't spend more time with them. This was the type of mother I wanted to be; a mother who spends quality time with her children.

I needed more time to learn than people without a learning disability (dyslexia) and who went to a mainstream school. Black children who were lucky enough to go to a mainstream school were taught to learn. Even if they were at the bottom of the class and experiencing racism (which many did), at least they were in a learning environment. They were taught not just to survive, but to thrive in society, according to their dreams and potential.

In a capitalist society, those at the pinnacle of the social structure thrive on making a profit with the help of the destitute working-class person who works like a servant without making any profit. After the Second World War, the British Government welcomed West Indians from their colonies to come to help rebuild the economy by offering them cheap labour. They didn't have to be educated to do these jobs that their children would one day inherit. Therefore, sending them to an ESN school would ensure that they grow up to become labours.

At the age of six years old, my the headmistress told my mother I was backward, and they sent me off to a special school. At this school, there was no curriculum, no structure, no learning that would help me to go to the next stage. I could not read or write when I left school; I could only work as a cleaner or a packer in a factory, jobs my children would also inherit in order to feed the deadly sin of capitalism.

They wanted me to remain at the bottom of the social hierarchy so those at the top could strive while I barely survive. Racism and capitalism function side by side.

Like Doctor Martin Luther King, I too have a dream that one day, a capitalist society will be a thing of the past; there will be no poor woman, and there will be no rich man, there will be absolute equality, and we will not be judged by our physical attribute but our inner qualities. Lastly, this new society will be one where every child will be greatly encouraged to achieve their full potential.

I ask,

"what did we come here to do"?

"We came here to love each other,

to take care of the planet and everything therein,

as we do our children"!

Once your eyes open,

it is up to you to find your way through the maze of life.

It doesn't matter why your eyes were closed.

Maisie Barrett

Chapter Eight
The Conclusion The Beginning

I have shared so much of my life story with you and, in conclusion, this part of the book demonstrates how I have evolved as a human being, as part of our infinite Universe that is forever expanding and developing. I have evolved and gained confidence though I am still working on my self-esteem. The education system deemed me to be dull and unintelligent, and I have believed this nearly all my life.

Let me start by saying that I know now that I am intelligent. I am intelligent enough to take full responsibility for my life, although I am aware that people with power, like the British education system and those who spend their lives scamming and getting in the way of other people's life journey, can greatly influence your life. However, it is up each person individually to decide whether or not to be a perpetual victim. I have chosen not to, because I just can't lie down and die so the enemy can claim victory. Once your eyes have been opened, it is up to you to find your way through the maze of life. It doesn't matter why your eyes were closed. What matters is that they are now opened and now you can see your pathway clearly, although, like me, you may be wounded.

On the journey of life, sometimes we are alone, and sometimes we are not. I am the only child of my mother and also I am a loner, so I am alone most of the time. You can be married with a large family and friends and still be a loner, but that is someone who is a natural loner or an introvert. I am an extravert. People have come in and out of my life like the oxygen we breathe in and the carbon dioxide we breathe out. Not everyone is meant to stay in your life. We meet, we learn lessons and we move on, while some stay on board. I never met that bosom friend who liked me unconditionally nor have I yet met a soulmate or twin-flame to love me eternally, although I am not saying it is too late to do so. As the saying goes, "where there's life there's hope".

When I met my soul-friend, I used to tell her she was lucky and how unlucky I was. It was like a horrible song in her ears because I said it so often. I am not sure when I stopped feeling unlucky because I don't feel that way any more; I feel quite blessed.

I used to tell my soul-friend she was lucky because she was the most intelligent person I had ever met. Her language was so sophisticated and, as for general knowledge, there was nothing she didn't know. I have a good command of general knowledge now and four degrees to my name.

Her sentences were a mixture of simple, complex and compound sentences and big words. The way she spoke, I could only dream of speaking like that, literally in a dream, but now this is the way *I* write and speak. It has become a reality and not a dream.

She had to be careful about what she said to me. I couldn't take a joke because I would take it personally. In addition, I was afraid to speak out just in case people laughed at me if I said nothing worth listening to. Now, I really do not care what people think about me, although I am often critical about myself because I aim for perfection. This is not a good attribute, but hey, who is perfect?

I was very quiet when I was with two or more people, and it looked like I was just staring at them, but they didn't know that I was searching for the words in my head to converse with them. Now, I am a public speaker, although sometimes I can be a little quiet where several people are gathered socially, but I can still have a laugh and a conversation with people I don't know.

I was always told that just from looking at me, people knew I didn't have any confidence. I therefore became a target for bullying but I always fought back. I just wasn't afraid of bullies. I guess for someone like me, who came from a backward school, to put them in their place was embarrassing, so they would just stay away. This happened to me at school. By the time I left, I had no friends. It was a mainstream school, so it was very difficult to fit in after spending eight years in a special school.

I felt rejected, both at school and at home. All my life, I felt rejected by my father, who only spoke to me when he was beating me, although he did speak to his other children from a different mother. My mother didn't talk to me either, so I grew up believing that no one loved me. Inevitably, then, I became a loner. And very depressed.

Loneliness was my life. I often personified it when writing poetry as an undergraduate student studying Caribbean Studies and Creative Writing. Loneliness was like a hole in my life, and I was always looking for ways to fill that hole. I thought having a husband and children was the perfect remedy, but I was wrong. It was a selfish thought because I had nothing to offer them, but I didn't know any better at the time. Also, because I couldn't read and write and had no confidence, it was difficult to get a job, so I was bored, penniless and lonely.

In 1989, I was this person I have been describing to you. However, I hope you will agree that I have evolved. It is now 2023, and I can tell you that the hole I had in my life is now full of peace and love. I can see a huge bright light at the end of the tunnel that goes on forever and ever.

Loneliness has been a thorn in my side since I was a child. But as Albert Einstein once wrote, "I live in that solitude which is painful in youth, but delicious in the years of maturity". This is how I feel today. My extended family is still not close to me, and I have very few friends. Moreover, I am single and still waiting for love to find me, but not to fill a hole in my life, because the hole I once had has disappeared. I am not alone because I have the gift of life and I appreciate the time I spend alone. I came to realise that life is precious when I thought I was going to die.

And thus, to conclude, I will share my final story with you that opened my eyes and helped me to appreciate life and stop having suicidal thoughts. Sometimes, something has to give you a big shake to wake you up so you can appreciate life. As the songwriter [Petula Clark] says, "Some are lucky, some are not. "Just be thankful for what you've got".

In my early twenties, when I met the man I thought would be my soulmate, I once tried to cut my wrist. B I just scratched the surface of my skin; I was only trying to get his attention. I still have the scars to remind me of my silly action. As a single mother of three, I used to go to bed thinking that the only solution to my silent pain and frustration was to commit suicide, which helped me relax before going to bed, although most nights, I went to bed drunk and that contributed to my relaxed state. I hated alcohol, so I would drink before going to bed, until I got used to it. Whenever there was a dilemma I had to face, the first thing that came into my mind were suicidal thoughts. However, in the twinkling of an eye, faster than a flash of lightning, just by chance, I stopped these negative thoughts because I thought I really was going to die.

I would never have taken my life. I believe that God game me life and only God can take it back. But this negative thought was destroying my aura and making me meet the wrong people. My reaction to life was a cry for help, except no one was listening to me because it was a silent cry, not even my mother heard it throughout her lifetime. This horrible feeling of depression was still apparent in my life when I started to have my children. They felt my pain, but they didn't know what was going on. They had their own cries that may have begun in my womb, because I was crying inside before they were born. They felt my pain, as children normally do when their parents are hurting, but they just can't explain it and my cries profoundly affected them.

In November 2021, I had a health scare. I thought I was going to die and the thought of dying made me realise that, no matter the obstacles in my life, I would rather be alive than dead. I wanted to live so I could carry on living my life to the fullest and be there for my children, my grandson and my god-daughter, who is named after me.

Night-time has always been my most sensitive time, especially when gazing up into the sky at midnight. I never closed my curtains because of my love for the sky and the Universe. In my mind's eye, as I lay back in my bed and looked up into a black, starless winter sky, I reminded myself that birds of all sizes and species can become prey to another animal, including humans. If I looked across the deep blue ocean, I saw that every fish has a predator. If I looked into the animal kingdom, I saw that even the lion has to watch its back and if I looked deep within the earth's soil, I saw that every creature is another creature's food.

Finally, I looked at the human kingdom and saw that, like the king of the jungle, the lion, there are both predators and prey and we all live side by side. We must all watch our backs and be careful as we journey through life together, making sure that there isn't a psychopath or some other social predator lurking about, such as the British education system. Nature may decide to show its anger when it breathes great thunderstorms upon the earth or creates an earthquake that suddenly comes like a thief in the night to shake us off our feet, forcing us to run away and leave our possessions behind, sometimes with fatal results. Nature is therefore both our predator and our protector because it also helps keep us alive by supplying us with fresh air, water and food.

I looked at our world and saw suffering in every corner, in the life of every individual at all levels. Though some people's pain is inconsequential to others, to them it is like having to climb the highest mountain in order to overcome it. I know that, as I take each single breath, a young child somewhere is made an orphan, or is born seriously deformed, while someone somewhere else is told that they have a few days or weeks to live. And not only did I feel guilty about all the years I had contemplated suicide, I felt guilty for asking God to heal my body when there is so much suffering in the world.

I am of the opinion that the suffering we see is just Mother Nature taking its course, doing what it was created to do by God's command because every kingdom is almost identical to one another in its suffering. This is because Mother Nature, or the Universe, is not prejudiced. That is why I say, it is not suffering; it is just the way it is. We are a part of an infinite Universe where there are explosions, births and the death of stars as the Universe expands and develops like every living thing on the earth, including the plants and the trees. And so we, too, are a part of that great expanding Universe as we evolve and develop as humans and as individuals.

I felt guilty and selfish for having suicidal thoughts all my life, and now that Mother Nature is taking its course, I suddenly wanted to live and beg its forgiveness. I felt ashamed to ask God to spare my life. Who am I? Aren't I the same and equal to everything that God has made upon the earth that must one day die and return to the Spirit World?

The Universe continues to strive and expand, and so do we humans. And as Mother Nature continues to take its course, God has given us the ability to live our lives to the fullest among the sufferings and diversities that we must face with the help of Mother Nature. We only have to reach out and believe because everything we need is there for us to take in abundance.

It takes a whole village to raise a child, but if that village fails the child, when the child grows up it can learn the rules of the Universe and (apart from the basic necessities of life that even the birds and the bees enjoy) can harvest far more in abundance and prosper like the rich and famous, but only if it's their heart's desire to improve their lives and mend the cracks beneath their feet caused by society, as I am trying to do. This is what I meant when I said that I take full responsibility for my life as an adult whose eyes are not open. Though wounded, I am trying to rejoin the pathway I was supposed to be travelling on.

We were born with the ability to manipulate the Universe in order to create the life we want, even though predators are looking and studying us from a distance. We can also heal ourselves if we believe in the magnificent powers that God has given us.

And thus, instead of praying, I gave God thanks for my life, believing I will live a long life. I gave God thanks for my healthy organs, my healthy body and my healthy skin, believing I am healed. I continue to affirm these healthy and positive desires as often as I can, each time I open my eyes and feel God's breath flowing through me, as I look up into the white morning sky.

I have come to understand that being born into a world of predators like the racist British Education System, the paedophiles, the abusers in our lives and also fatal storms, the list is exhaustive, helps us learn the skills to develop, survive and protect ourselves, and make a difference in a forever changing Universe in order to live and achieve success.

Animals are beautiful, perfect creatures, but we have one thing over them; we can change our world to limit unnecessary suffering and create more space so every individual can develop to their full potential. Therefore, in the human kingdom, predators that cause severe damage in society must either be put in prison or they must be exposed. My aim is to expose my predators more widely than they have already been exposed; I have the intelligence to do so by writing this book and writing a musical play.

The act of exposing something or someone aligns with the rules of the Universe and Mother Nature because you reap what you sow (cause and effect) for everyone to see. The Universe will grant your heart's desire, whether it be negative or positive. So, you have to be careful what you think and say and in what you do.

The British government wanted Caribbean people to come to England to help rebuild the economy. The Universe granted this wish, even though the government had evil intentions for the children of these Caribbean people. The racist British education system deliberately placed black children who had average or above average intelligence in special schools for children who were deemed to have low intelligence, to be taught by unqualified teachers. The plan was to make these innocent children labourers like their parents, even if their destiny was to become doctors. This is what the government sowed in the Universe until it was exposed by the Honourable Bernard Coard and the documentary by Steve McQueen Subnormal: A British Scandal. Hopefully, justice will be done when the government has to pay out compensation for the damage it has caused to the lives of the people who were suppressed by the British education system. But even if the government refuses to pay us compensation, the documentary Subnormal: A British Scandal, this book and the stories of others affected by what it did will continue to expose it until the law grants us justice one day – if it ever does.

If any member of society tries to suppress you, or someone else's tragedy affects you, like the way my life affected my children, you can still change your life for the better, if you have the desire to do so, and you believe and work towards it; as I did and, indeed, am still doing. You see, like the Universe, my dreams and ambitions have no end. I am a natural humanitarian and activist, so I think beyond my needs, which extend to my community and beyond. I am here to make a significant positive difference before I return to the Spirit World. There, I have written it down and so shall it be.

It was my heart's desire to go to Africa and I did go there, although it wasn't my destiny to stay. It was my desire to go to university, despite hardly being able to read or write or have a worthwhile conversation with anyone and, with hard work, I accomplished this desire. I ultimately hoped to tell the world my story and look, here I am sharing it with you right now! I have achieved all my goals up to this point. When I went to the British Embassy in Africa, they told me that they couldn't help me to return to England because I wasn't British, although I was born in England. When I left the building, I made a promise to myself that one day I would stand in the House of Commons and demand why. On March 2023, I gave a talk in the House of Commons and mentioned how I was treated in the British Embassy in 1989. It has always been my ambition to get involved in government actives. I joined the Labour Party on May 13, 2023.

And so the day shall come when my children, their offspring and I shall shine brightly like the silver stars in the heavens, and shine like the golden sun and the moon, as a healthy and prosperous family. We will have total peace and success one day. We will leave all the misfortunes and struggles, chiefly caused by society, behind us through our determination, the manipulation of the Universe and God's support. My career as an author has just started, and I will be financially secure and debt-free one day. There, I have written it down and so shall it be.

> I hope my story will make a positive difference in someone's life
>
> in the same way other people's stories have helped me to grow and become my better self.
>
> The racist British Education System tried to change my destiny and bad parenting,
>
> but I reclaimed it by recreating it.
>
> Thank you for reading my book! When you have finished,
>
> please give it to someone who needs encouragement
>
> to reach out and take their birthright
>
> to happiness and success.

The subject of book two has nothing to do with my story.

Nevertheless, I have added it because more than thirty years ago

it was in the father of my children's country

that I wrote to my mother and because I struggled to write;

I promised myself that one day that I would learn to read and write properly

and tell my story to the world.

Three decades later to the date, once more it was in his homeland.

that I decided to write a letter to the African heads of state,

because I was confident that I could

and I did not struggle to write it.

Part II

Dear African Leaders

A UNITED AFRICA
IS THE FUTURE

START TRADING WITH
EACH OTHER MORE

Maisie Barrett

"Africa will furnish a development of civilization which the world has never yet witnessed. Its great peculiarity will be its moral element."

Edward Wilmot Blyden (1832 -1912)

PART II

The Letters

Dear African Leaders
A United Africa Is The Future
Start Trading With Each Other More

DEDICATION

To My Ancestors
The Better Half Snatched From The Bosom of Mother Africa

Dear Leaders of Africa

I greet you in the name of Africa, the land of the rich, golden, fertile soil of the Garden of Eden, where the First Man and Woman were created and formed by the Breath of the Spirit of the Living God, responsible for everything that exists in our Great Universe, including the Universe itself.

I am writing to you because I love and care about Africa and its people. I would like to see a United States of Africa, where African leaders are united on all grounds of the social, economic and political discourse, activities, planning and trading within Africa. If you do not unite, the African people will never be respected, wherever they live throughout the diaspora.

Though African countries successfully gained independence, the continent has remained divided and the issues have continued, so much so that, on 9 July 2002, when the Organisation of African Unity (OAU) had run its course and was replaced by the African Union (AU), the same agenda applied to 'encourage political and economic integration among member states, and to eradicate colonialism and neo-colonialism from the African continent'. How ignorant was I? I thought colonialism had ended when the African countries gained their independence.

When we call for a United States of Africa, we echo the words of Kwame Nkrumah, the first President of the first independent African country, when he said, 'unite now or perish' and he called for a

United Sates of Africa, naming Kinshasa as the capital. It seems as though an African Revolution will be the last resort to unite Africans.

I agree with Kwame that the meeting place to discuss the unification of Africa should have been held in the Democratic Republic of Congo (DRC). The year is now 2022, and we still feel strongly that the conference should take place in DRC when you take into consideration that 'by the early 1900s the kingdom of Congo was sliced into pieces (at the time of the scramble for Africa) and the rainforest of the Congo river basin was one of the most brutally exploited places on earth' (Robert Harms, *Land of Tears*). The positive media exposure to its vast, rich, gigantic landscape will generate great economic benefits and awareness of this beautiful country whose resources feed the world today.

Before I continue with Kwame's prediction of what would happen if Africa did not unite in his lifetime, let me remind you that, on 25 May 1963, the OAU was established in order to unite Africa and resolve all issues caused by Europeans during the slave trade and colonial rule. Thirty-two signatory governments put pen to paper, and the OAU was ready to get to work to tackle the main problems on the continent. At the very first conference, Alieu Ebrima Cham Joof had this to say:

"It is barely 75 years when the European Powers sat round the table in Germany each holding a dagger to carve up Africa for its own benefit.…Your success will inspire and speed up the freedom and total independence of the African continent and eradicate imperialism and colonialism from the continent and eventually neo-colonialism from the globe…

Your failure, which no true African in Africa is praying for, will prolong our struggle with bitterness and disappointment. I therefore adjure that you ignore any suggestion outside Africa and holding that the present civilization, which some of the big powered are boasting of, sprang up from Africa, and realising that the entire world has something earthly to learn from Africa, you would endeavour your utmost to come to agreement, save Africa from the clutches of neo-colonialism and resurrect African dignity, manhood and national stability."[i]

The speech was delivered in 1963. In 2002, the OAU was replaced with the AU and it was unbelievable to discover that some of the key aims of the OAU were still on the political agenda for 2002, despite the members having had nearly 30 years to resolve Africa's socio-economic and political situation.

Returning to Kwame's advice for the unification of Africa when he declared that Africa would perish if it did not unite: the European colonisers knew what they were doing. They would never have allowed Africa to perish to the extent that they and future generations could not continue to exploit African resources.

The plan was that Africa would continuously experience severe socio-economic and political problems, due to the legacies of enslavement, colonisation and the impregnation of their cultures, politics and mentality, while, as colonisers, they would continue to dictate how Africa is governed, even if dictatorship went against an African way of life, which it did, and still does today.

Furthermore, they were also fully aware that even if Africa should one day gain independence, due to the aforementioned legacies, Africans would still depend on Europeans. This belief was also used by white abolitionists in order to persuade the various European governments to end enslavement throughout the Americas. European governments believed and predicted that black people would never amount to anything as a people or nations, so why not end their bondage?

After the abolition of slavery, the next European hegemony was to colonise the Motherland in order to continue milking her breast like one does a cow, but this was a short-lived methodology in the 1960s, which finally witnessed African independence. Europeans saw this coming through the constant wars against colonialism, so they devised not one, but several ways to continue the suppression of African people. They placed a debt upon their heads for the building of an infrastructure that the natives did not ask them to build. Thousands of Africans protested against Europeans building on their lands, according to Robin Walker, the author of *When We Ruled*.

Furthermore, Africans were forced to pay colonial taxes, which was a ludicrous, narcissistic, and psychopathic act. Until that debt is paid off, Europeans can automatically confiscate Africa's national reserves. A website called Answer Africa published an article titled *The 14 Countries Who Still Pay Colonial Tax to France*. The article shared what amounts to a criminal act on humanity, namely that France earns 400 billion from the African continent. A very insightful article by Anastacia Promskaya in 2015, first published by Uhuru News, has this to say:

"...the former president of France, Jacques Chirac said the French people should accept the fact that a large amount of the money in their banks comes precisely from the exploitation of former colonies on the African continent.

France claims the right to exploit any natural resource discovered in the country. France claims it has the first right to buy any natural resources found on the territory of its ex-colonies. The African countries are also not allowed to seek other partners freely.

France forces African countries to give preference to French interests and companies in the field of public procurement and public biding.

According to government contracts, French companies must be considered first. Only after that can Africans connect with other foreign companies. It doesn't matter if the African countries would benefit from a partner outside of France.

As a consequence, in many French ex-colonies all the major economic assets are in French hands. For example, in Côte d'Ivoire French companies own and control all the major utilities – water, electricity, telephone, transport, ports and major banks. The same situation exists in the field of commerce, construction and agriculture.

France claims an exclusive right to supply military equipment and training to African military officers.

Through a sophisticated scheme of scholarships, grants and "defence agreements" attached to the Colonial Pact (the document that sets up the common currency for all Francophone countries – the

CFA Franc), African countries send their senior military officers for training in France."

In 1958 in Guinea, when Sekou Toure wisely decided to take back his country from French colonial rule, the angry, childlike French destroyed the country's infrastructure as much as they could before they left. They demolished buildings such as schools, nurseries, public offices and administration buildings. Then they went on to destroy cars, books, machines and so on.

Notwithstanding, what was more disturbing (and is evidence that France always had evil intentions for Africa from the outset), the so-called civilised French slaughtered horses and cows, poisoned food and burnt down food warehouses to ensure that the native Guineans would starve to death. In addition to all this, according to Anastacia Promskaya, before they left they "...trained and nourished hundreds, even thousands of traitors, when France needs them to commit another coup d'état or create a disturbing political situation inside Africa". Let us be realists, there are traitors in every corner of the world, not just in Africa.

I kindly ask the readers of this letter, before making a judgement and accusing our dear African leaders of corruption, to educate yourselves about Africa. I urge you to read the article by Anastacia Promskaya.

A recent article dated October 2018, written by Jubilee Debt Campaign and titled *Africa's Growing Debt Crises: Who is the Debt Owed To?*, explains that due to the colonial debts, it is not surprising that Africa is getting deeper and deeper into further debt, coupled with corruption, in order to survive:

African government external debt payments have increased dramatically in the last few years. Between 2015 and 2017 they doubled, rising from a (mean, unweighted) average of 5.9% of government revenue in revenue 2015, to 11.8% of government revenue in 2017. This means African government debt payments are at the highest level since 2001. Key causes of this dramatic change are increases in lending since 2008 from multiple lenders followed by falls in commodity prices in mid-2014, and rising US dollar interest rates and the value of the US dollar in recent years.

Now, as for the United Kingdom, the Guardian online informs us that 24 nations, including Sudan, Somalia and Zimbabwe, owe the United Kingdom £2.34 billion; and £825 million of that is interest. Tim Jones, the senior policy officer (the first world) and a member of the pressure group at the Jubilee Debt Campaign, is calling for an end to 'third world debt'.

I am of the opinion that, like manufactured goods, slave traders, colonialists and slave masters throughout the Americas manufactured Black Behaviour and Black Suicide, in such a way that no matter where they live, as long as they were once enslaved or colonised by Europeans, their behaviour and mentality towards themselves and to Europeans are the same or identical. In this instance, we are referring to political and religious wars and conflict, and poverty in the Black World. This list also includes racial hatred and those who would rather have children outside their own race or who are of dual heritage, to create a lighter, "acceptable" skin tone.

There are often wars in Africa between Africans, and let us not forget about the black on black crime in America and England, where a black youth can smash a bottle in the face of another youth, for no reason at all.

Apparently, a white professor of psychology at the University of Chicago proclaimed this prophesy to the world:

"Give me a dozen healthy infants, well-informed, and my own specified world to bring them up in, and I'll guarantee to take any one at random and train him to become any type of specialist. I might select doctor, lawyer, artist, merchant, chief, and yes beggar man and thief, regardless of his talents, penchants, tendencies, abilities vocations and the race of this ancestors.". (Watson 1924,cited in Wright, 1984)

Could this have been the plan when white colonial rulers met around the table in Berlin, Germany to discuss the peaceful partition of Africa: to turn black Africans into beggars? It is obvious that they devised a programme designed to create perpetual division and wars among black people in Africa and throughout the diaspora, while blacks continued to depend on, serve and meet the economic needs of Europeans, while their own needs were, and still are, unmet. They have turned Africa into nations of beggars, though Africa should be the richest continent in the word due to its abundance of natural resources.

In Africa and in the countries of the descendants of the kidnapped Africans even today, there is fighting and killing amongst them in more ways than one; for example, even as they try to live peacefully with whites and to protect their own interests, to the extent that blacks are accusing other blacks of racism, if they dare to highlight institutional racism at all levels and try to explain white superiority. When slavery is mentioned, many blacks would rather blame Africans than whites. Marcus Garvey called this behaviour mental slavery, due to the effects of the brainwashing, racist theories of pseudo science, coupled with general and religious education, or failure to educate.

Today, Black Scientists have classified this behaviour as 'mentacide', which was developed to combat the rising level of consciousness and black nationalism of the '60s and '70s, which threatened the process of European world domination. Black Scientists go on to explain that the confusion is caused by the "powerful, yet subtle, white concepts of 'free will' that teaches the victim that they have a choice they can make, suggesting therefore we black people must be held responsible for the consequences that occur in our lives, for example the poverty and political chaos in Africa. Black people are held responsible for slavery, and colonialism and all the social problems that stems from Europeans conquests". (Bobby E Wright (1984))

The converted Christians today are still convinced that the social and economic problems of Africa are a direct result of God's punishment for idolatry. These Christians are unaware that ancient and modern Europeans, from the 1400s onwards, also worshipped different gods and committed evil and atrocious offences against the people they conquered throughout Africa and the Americas. Nevertheless, their countries continue to prosper economically today, with the help of black taxpayers and taxes on debts in their ex-colonial countries.

To conclude, in the discussions between Black Scientists and Christian believers, the time has come for Africans and the Caribbean heads of state to invest more in science and less in religion. With respect to Christians leaders, I truly believe that Africa and the world would live in more harmony and peace without religion. This is what Mrs Betty Akeredolu, the wife of the Ondo State Governor, has asserted to Nigerians (although she should have included all the African countries), She writes:

"It is glaring that the foreign religions over which we are killing ourselves in Nigeria have failed the world in this season of anomie and only science can save mankind."

"Indeed, Coronavirus has humbled the world's religions and Nigerians whose lives depend on praying and fasting for miracles to happen in this digital world of science and technology."

"When I said that I was more than convinced that religion is man-made and a bastion of sexism, which has subjugated women, festered gender inequality, stifled progressive thinking, retarded development and invariably added little or no value to our lives, I was called unprintable names."

"I remain unshakeable with my conviction."

"This virus has proved me right, to a large extent. Nigerians, in particular, have invested so much in religion that amounted to nothing."

I discovered a post on social media of children putting their hands on a map, as they prayed for the world to heal from coronavirus, yet black people are being forced out of their homes in China, exposing them to the virus even more. The Chinese do not care about the people of Africa, but they do care about Africa's resources and land and want to protect it by increasing their military presence in Africa. An online article by Nyshka Chandran claims that:

"China is looking to strengthen defence engagement with African countries, adding to its economic and commercial profile on the continent."

"That would complement existing Chinese ventures, such as peace sales, as well as protecting Chinese assets, experts say."

The western world continues to benefit from African migration because it invests in businesses and education, while the borders created by Europeans still divide Africa, which helps to force Africans to migrate to the countries of their ex-colonisers, in order to continue to enrich their economies, while Africa remains divided and people live in poverty and amidst wars.

When all is said and done, it is not too late for us to be united. Like the honourable Julius Malema, the South African Pan Africanist and politician, and many great Pan Africanists before him, we are still pleading to you, our leaders, to break down all foreign borders designed by colonial invaders and simultaneously keep out European governments whose intention it is to colonise Africa again.

Angélique Kidjo, a Beninese singer-songwriter and actress, known for her diverse musical influences and creative music videos, asserted confidently in an interview that, "Africa is the only part of the world where you have growth". She says, "Europe is sinking and, in my opinion, Brexit does not help the situation".

A Nigerian female activist overtly accused the French President, Emmanuel Macron, of spreading terrorism in Nigeria and other African countries. She is convinced that the French action is hinged on economic benefits, in order to continue to exploit northern Nigeria, in particular the Lake Chad basin, which, it is no surprise to establish, is the poorest part of the country.

This strong, fearless and confident woman, Nana Yaa Asantewaa (1850-1921), warns the President that Nigerians are not prepared to be colonised again and reminds him that France would be a third world country if not for its continuous exploitation of Africa; in fact, the western world would be a dump if it could not feed on Africa's resources. This Nigerian woman went on to declare that she is speaking on behalf of all Africans, because the land belongs to Africans. Let us remember this, leaders of Africa: not only must African territory be protected, but its resources must stay in Africa for the benefit of African people.

In 1884-1885, European vultures sat around the Berlin Conference table to discuss the partition of Africa, and they discussed how they would turn Africans into beggars, with a high suicide rate and being constantly at war with each other. In addition, the plan was for the European countries to peacefully divide the different African countries among themselves, in order to avoid war between them, regardless of how this would affect the natives. Though the plan was successful, it did not stop them from fighting each other with the help of some African natives. It was pure hysteria and chaos on African soil (A. Diouf, 2003), with Africans fighting each other, Europeans fighting each other and Africans fighting Europeans. I am of the opinion that colonisation was a genocide programme designed to take the place of the slave trade. Thousands of Africans lost their lives as a result of slavery and thousands more would continue to lose their lives through civil wars, poverty and migration right up until the present day, as a direct result of slavery and colonial legacies.

Ten European countries were invited to the conference. America was also invited, but declined the invitation, because America did not want to build an empire in Africa. Out of ten invitations, only seven European government officials were present at the genocide event. It was an utter disgrace and shameful to Africa that, at the time when the conference for the scramble for Africa took place, the only people who were not invited to sit around the table were Africans.

The unification of Africa is of utmost urgency. Let us start by building and maintaining perpetual political relationships and continuous discourse bringing positive outcomes among yourselves. The plea for a united Africa should be portrayed in education at all levels, in the media, tabloid papers, artwork, songs, films, and sports.

African leaders, in addition to this, there is an urgent need to encourage a rapid flow of migration within, and to, Africa to help make Africa great again. The recent social unrest that took place in South Africa, where natives were fighting and protesting against black Africans from other African countries taking their jobs (but note that they did not fight the whites or Asian people) must not happen again. How backward was that? It was an utter shame. Such social unrest does not happen in England any more. After the First World War, when Africans and Caribbean soldiers were demobilised in England, English natives took to the streets to protest that black people were taking their jobs. A similar race riot occurred in England after the

Second World War, when black people from around the world and Asians were asked to come to help rebuild the economy, but they were greeted with tremendous hostility and racism. The white natives of Britain were also worried that the migrants would take their jobs.

Referring back to the situation in South Africa, this is what an African from Zimbabwe had to say about his personal experience of living in South Africa as an African migrant:

Dear African Leaders

I am a male adult aged 45 years, and l reside in South Africa. To use the term 'dear' to address you all will be an understatement. There is nothing warm to embrace in this entire letter about any warmth in the way l should address you all!

I am a Zimbabwean citizen who moved to South Africa to look for livelihood, not "green pastures" as some misuse terminology as flattery. This is an ideally serious issue knowing my mind. I arrived in South Africa as a forced refugee in 2007 as things had turned politically nasty in Zimbabwe which was then under the leadership of a quasi-military dictator Robert Mugabe. I ran away from political persecution just like many other youths seeking freedom, education and jobs which were promised during election campaign but never materialised. I had no passport, and no visa to be allowed entry into South Africa as the law would obviously require. But anyway the dog-eat-dog situation forced me and several others to border jump and enter South African territory through the several illegal entry points where payment of bribes has been tacitly normalized by thepowers that be. I paid my 1000 Rands, which l had saved for months on end working as a gardener at a consulate of one of the European Union countries in Harare Zimbabwe.

I was left with only 500 Rands to live on and probably utilize for the unknown transport costs and food that awaited me on my determined journey to go and work in unknown territory. We walked steadily for an entire night after crossing Beitbridge border post through an illegal entry point, and I managed to get to Messina town 25 km away. Some of the ladies we had on our group were left behind at these several illegal security check points and I later on got information that they had to exchange or buy passage from the security forces through sex as some did not have money to pay bribes! I also learned of a woman who was married but still received a similar treatment from the soldiers!

Anyway after I arrived in Messina town we were fortunate to find transport to Pretoria where I had a friend waiting for me to take me in and probably find work for me at his construction workplace. We were now only 9 of us left as others had taken different directions, as we proceeded with the journey. We were bundled into a truck and a tent thrown to hide us from view and the long journey of 500km began to Pretoria. We paid 200 Rand each for the journey, but the unfortunate part is that after travelling 200 or so kilometres, the truck driver was stopped by police and each one of us again had to part with 100 rand for police bribes, so we could pass on. We had not eaten anything for two days now and the driver would hear none of our pleas for a short recess.

We arrived in Pretoria Bosman station around 5pm when the real trouble began! A plain clothes policeman had been waiting for us at exactly the place we were dropped off and your guess is as good as mine, we had to part with more money. I slept on the streets in a foreign country as my phone's battery had finished, and I had been foolish enough not to write down my friend's number on a piece of paper for reference should such a calamity occur!

I knew nobody around and had even lost sense of direction, so l decided to pick a corner spot near a takeaway shop sit down to plan my next move. As l sat there pondering, a group of men wearing overalls passed by me talking and laughing in my language. I became excited to hear someone from my home country.

I walked over to the group as they stopped at an intersection to cross the road, and l grabbed the attention of one of the guys with my nervous approach. Philip was his name may he be blessed forever! After relaying my ordeal to him, he didn't think twice but grabbed my bag as if l was his long lost friend, and invited me to go with him to his place of lodging in Tembisa, a high density location in Johannesburg. To cut a long story short Philip is the one who provided food, lodgings and transport money for me for a whole month before l could finally get to Newcastle town in KwaZulu Natal where l was united with my friend.

I had simplified my understanding of South Africa and thought it was going to be pie in pie to get a job and live happily ever after, but l had been grossly wrong. Life in South Africa was tough, as l later realized. Anything you want you'd have to pay for it. And even to have someone direct you to a job. As soon as you get it, you'd have to ' thank' them.

It didn't matter if it was a friend who found you the job. As l did not have papers but still needed a job, we had no option but to use the money to buy security officers certificates, so l could get employed as a security officer. Which l found would be the simplest employment opportunity in South Africa if you are an undocumented foreigner. I also bought a fake passport to tally with my fake qualification and was quickly snapped up by one security company in Newcastle. The interview had been very brief. They wanted to know my real name, not the one on the passport. My heart skipped a bit and this lady who was the owner of the company didn't look surprised at all, as to what she was asking me. She even said I know you're Zimbabwean and all the papers I was holding mean nothing to her, as she is aware that they're all fake, but since she liked what she termed my reasonableness she would give me a job at an isolated place where inspectors will never come to verify anything somewhere at a mine dumping site in the hills 10 km out of town where I can stay there and only talk to my supervisor, as and when he managed to come for Officers visits. I worked for 6 years for this company at this one mine site and only saw this lady owner as and when they visited this site once during upgrades of contracts.

One day word was brought by the supervisor that things had changed, and the site contract had been revoked and once again I was on the streets. Without documentation it proved difficult for me, but one day I got a job in a shop owned by a Chinese couple. And as I was cleaning I picked up a south African identity document in the flower beds, and it had a Chinese name and what probably sounded like a Zulu surname. It had the Chinese woman's face and looked very original. It caught me by surprise and I decided to ask her when I took it back to her. She became very angry and took the document but stated that I should not come back to work at her shop again the following day. Did I see something that I shouldn't have seen? I thought to myself. This was now 2013 around February. I had already spent 6 years in South African territory sending money back home through bus drivers and friends as my status was still questionable.

Newcastle was less tremulous than other cities in terms of police raids on foreign nationals and strict identity checks. I asked a friend how a Chinese couple could be citizens of South Africa, yet myself an African could not acquire an identity document despite several attempts at home affairs to legalize my status, which had been put now as refugee as they had offered me a 'simple' option or deportation. Should I further make objections or continue to appeal their reasoning?

My friend laughed at my argument, and simply shrugged and said to me, why I was not aware of the new world philosophy, to buy my own Identity document, just like everyone else was doing, including that identity document that, cost my job at the Chinese shop. And so, I began to realise that, unless I could afford to pay 15 000 Rands, I would never be able to formalize my status in South Africa.

It is now 2020, I am still do not have South African citizenship. Therefore, I played hide and seek with the immigration department, although I have been living in the country for 14 years. I have contributed immensely to the country's GDP growth, as I am now working in tourism, and the outflow in the touring industry is just too huge to ignore its contributions to the South African economy, but still I always walk out of their office buildings with my head held low, as I continue being sent from pillar to post over the formalization of my status in order to have recognition of my work towards building this economy.

It has been very frustrating despite knowing what's happening in the scenes behind.

Am now opting to move overseas should an opportunity arise. And I am currently making frantic efforts to leave Africa and its bureaucratic elements, which do not serve a nation's interest but personal ego.

Yours sincerely

Edwin

Dear African Leaders

African leaders, this heartfelt story makes my heart rage with anger and burning frustration since, if it were not for colonisation, Edwin, a Zimbabwean, would not have been a foreigner in South Africa. The earlier map of Africa clearly shows that the people of these two countries were one people. Moreover, such behaviour and mentality were not a part of African way of life.

The part of Edwin's story that resonates with me is when he asked his friend:

"...how a Chinese couple could be a citizen of South Africa yet myself an African could not acquire an identity document despite several attempts at home affairs to legalize my status, which had been put now as refugee, as they had offered me a 'simple' option or deportation should I further make objections or continue to appeal their reasoning."

African leaders: break down all borders created by Europeans and thereafter either implement or amend immigration laws to welcome diversity and migration within Africa, at all times. After all, scientists teach us that 'Africa is by far the most genetically diverse continent', according to BBC News Africa. Let us celebrate our differences among one people and unite.

We need talented, skilled and creative African people from all over the world to migrate to the various African countries that need their services the most, instead of migrating to Europe, America and England, where they are often not welcomed or allowed entry for economic reasons. It is also fundamental that the government should endeavour to support those talented and industrious African geniuses, who are privileged enough to be able to migrate to other countries, yet have decided to remain living in Africa to help enrich their own economies.

African migration to Africa will be for the betterment of the continent, in the same way that African migration (or should I say, black presence) in America, Canada, France, England and throughout Europe (especially after the First and Second World Wars) has greatly benefited the economies of those countries, which will continue in the same way if African governments do not tackle the very root of all African problems forthwith.

We need great leaders like yourselves to love and put the interests of Africa and Africans first on the agenda of political discourse, planning and building. If we do not love ourselves as a race, why should other people respect us, or even care about us? It is globally acknowledged that Europeans only love our resources. They give us aid to hold on to our resources. They keep us poor, just to hold on to our resources. It is not out of charity or love. They simply do not care about Africans. Angélique Kidjo brought this reality to the world's attention, when she said:

"Ebola has existed for the past 20 years, why doesn't anybody come up with a vaccination? The pharmaceutical firms they knew about it. As long as it is in Africa, nobody cares..."

This is how much Bill Gates cares about Africa. He declaresd that: "We must depopulate Africa to save Europe". Mr Gates has either forgotten or is not aware that Africa feeds the world.

Therefore, Africa's future depends on you, the leaders. Let there be a meeting (on African soil) to discuss how the African governments can work together to help unite and rebuild Africa and do away with Europeanisation that is not conducive to African personality, way of life or the environment.

According to Nigerian President Buhari, western culture is destroying African values and Chinese culture will also influence the way Africans think. In saying this, we are also aware that we can learn something useful from all cultures, but it must be absolutely beneficial to Africa and its people. We need to eliminate colonialism in every shape or form and focus more on African cultures and spirituality.

Mother Africa needs to return to the African System, which was a social system where the people prospered equally and more peacefully, as it was before European encroachment upon the continent. However, I am not saying that there was absolute peace in Africa, but the historical fact is that Africa was a more peaceful place to live than the western world at the beginning of the 1400s. European slave traders and colonial leaders have acknowledged this assertion in their literature. They have also declared that the socio-economic and political chaos that we see in Africa today started at the time of the slave trade, which, in turn, laid down the foundation for the development of the colonial wars on African soil.

Africans must be their own aid in the development of their nations because they are rich enough to do it. According to the media, the ten poorest African countries are: Burundi, Malawi, Niger, Mozambique, the Central African Republic, Madagascar, Liberia,

Gambia, Guinea and the Democratic Republic of Congo. This last country is the second largest country among them and will require more aid from the more peaceful and wealthier countries to help combat poverty. However, having said that, it is imperative to highlight the contradictory fact that the African continent is unimaginably rich, and Congo DRC is said to be the richest among all the countries. It is apparent that Congo can feed the whole world until the year 2050, and yet of its 77 million population, 80% live in extreme poverty. Therefore, it is obvious that Congo's natural resources are being used to feed the world, but there is not enough for the Congolese people, and coupled with the political problems, they are forced to migrate to the countries that caused the problems in the first place.

What has Congo got that the western world desperately and literally needs to survive, and to maintain world power? According to Kambale Musavuli from Friends of the Congo, along with its $24 trillion in raw minerals, Congo has 10% of the world's copper, 30% of the world's diamonds, 70% of the world's cotton and 50% of the world's cobalt.

Musavuli informs us that Congo is the number one producer of cobalt. For those readers who do not know what cobalt is used for, there is a high chance that our batteries, cars, phones, televisions and all electrical equipment used today contain cobalt from the Congo, but Musavuli reminds us that 'no one knows about this'. In addition, cobalt is also used for aeroplanes and space shuttles that Musavuli blames for the havoc around the world when it could be put to better use in Congo and throughout Africa.

https://youtu.be/mxa4YbmMkQ0

African leaders, I urge you to get around the table to talk about protecting Africa's natural resources. It is obvious why Britain is prepared to break away from the EU, Britain's closest trading neighbours and, therefore, cheaper to trade with, according to a rule of economics that is called the Gravity Rule. Although African nations are England's most distant trading partners, it is cheaper to trade with African countries because they are not negotiating the right price. At present, England negotiates trading relationships with the countries of the EU that it has left, but has declared that this political and economic move will not interfere with how it trades with Africa! Well, I am not surprised.

After Brexit, there is an opportunity for trade growth between Commonwealth countries. The UK government has said that increasing economic, political and other ties with Commonwealth member countries is an important priority. Our member countries are all committed to deepening trade integration in the Commonwealth as part of the Commonwealth's prosperity agenda.[ii]

Therefore, I ask you to negotiate with European governments, who depend on African resources, to buy these resources at a price which takes into account the needs of African people on the continent of Africa. Also, African leaders, do not continue to be bullied and treated as slaves. You should have a right to sell to whom you wish and using African currency, not European.

As a historian, let me remind you that before the invasion of Africa by Europeans, we used to help and share our time and resources with each other and our neighbouring countries, according to the African way of life. Every African was his brother's and sister's keeper. We lived in co-operative communities like a large family and, even today, every adult is an aunty or an uncle. The larger countries often helped the smaller ones to fight their battles, even in colonial wars, when Europeans were fighting each other on African soil for their portion of Africa (A. Diouf, 2003). We traded both with each other and with foreigners. We also travelled to neighbouring countries to work, which benefited each community equally. Europeans were convinced that we were enslaving each other; however, they were interpreting African communities based on Roman slave societies that had helped shape their own world.

In addition to the above, everyone had a roof over their heads and lived on land that belonged to all who lived on it. There was no homelessness as we see in Africa today. During and after the slave trade, African people began experiencing homelessness, just like in Europe. Private land ownership was a European custom that was brought to Africa when a law was implemented in the 19th century introducing rights to private ownership of land. Apparently, it took some time for Africans to get used to individuals owning their land.

Furthermore, unless there was a famine, everyone had food to eat. There was no starvation, therefore there were no beggars, nor thieves, because everyone had enough of the basic necessities of life to meet their daily needs (Lynch, 1971:171). A Nigerian enslaved African, Olaudah Equiano (1745-1810), also asserted in his autobiography, written after he had bought his freedom, that there was no need for beggars or thieves in Africa before Europeanisation (Lynch, 1971:172). I am not saying that I believe that everything was perfect in Africa. Like every society, there would have been people who committed minor offences and serious crimes, just for the sake of it. However, in Africa it happened far less frequently than in the western world, and European slave traders have admitted this.

In nearly every country on the continent, the main belief was Ubuntu, meaning 'humanity to others'. I am because we are. It is for this reason that I have often used the pronoun 'we' in this letter, which symbolises 'one people', 'one Africa'.

The pronoun 'we' represents a whole. We were the first to bring this concept to the world when we migrated and travelled out of Africa during the Ice Age; a concept the new natives of the western world must have forgotten, as they lived in their new harsh, icy environment. A concept that created a voluntary workforce in Africa where individuals worked for the whole community, so everyone benefited from the work of all the individuals who participated. African economies and way of thinking resembled communism, which Europeans have detested until this very day. The way Africans structured their economies was similar to the pyramid scheme based on a business model that many western entrepreneurs are members of today. The pyramid model has its origin in Africa, for example Egypt and Sudan, but it has been Europeanised. The way the scheme works is that each member depends on the other member to grow financially; therefore, there is no jealousy or corruption, because they work and share their ideas as a community.

When Europeans switched to trading in people, instead of African produce, in the 1300s in Europe there was no evidence that there were communities were based on a co-operative way of living. There was certainly no evidence of voluntary work that the whole village benefited from. The western world was completely opposite to African co-operative communities. It was based on slavery, egotism, greed, power, control and corruption that Africans have since imitated, which is one of the problems of Africa – Europeanisation.

In Europe, 'the rural population lived bound to hereditary service. Some peasants had the chance to improve their position, but far more lived an existence barely above the beasts of the field. They laboured partly to benefit the priests and monks whose role it was to serve Christ, but chiefly for the benefit of a powerful aristocracy of warriors' (Lacey & Danziger, 1999: 45, 210, 211).

Therefore, the natives of Europe were either royalty, landowners, free peasants or slaves. According to history, it was often difficult to distinguish the slaves from the free peasants, who worked on the land and paid rent and taxes to the landlord. When the land was sold, these free peasants were sold with the land, so the true reality was that they were also slaves.

As Africans, let us appreciate the ancient teaching of Ubuntu. I am because we are; where it takes a village to raise a child. The enslaved African took this belief to the slave land. When my mother was growing up in the 1920s in Jamaica, if she was seen behaving inappropriately when outdoors, a passer-by could punish her. By the time she arrived home, her parents would already have heard the news and would be very upset with her but grateful to the stranger.

We are the only people blessed with such a mentality, because we were the First Race, responsible for the birth of all races. The African race is the Parent Race and, as parents, we know how to love, share, care, nurture, and forgive everyone else but ourselves.

The development of the continent can easily be achieved with the help and aid of all the African

Leaders (they are rich enough, as I said before) and also the Africans who live everywhere except Africa. Do not forget the Better Half that was snatched from the bosom of Mother Africa. I am referring to African people who spread throughout the Caribbean and its basin and America, who now live in England, Canada and Europe. They have nearly 700 years of experience and much needed talents and skills that they have gained while living in the West.

I will continue to reiterate the need to encourage African migration from within throughout this letter to you. The skilled African who is planning to migrate to the western hemisphere to improve his or her life will only help to further enrich the western countries. China is also a main destination for Africans. Africans spend a fortune on education. According to the UNESCO Institute of Statistics, 'the US and UK host around 40,000 African students a year. China surpassed this number in 2014, making it the second most popular destination for African students studying abroad after France, which hosts just over 95,000 students'. According to an online article by Victoria Breeze and Nathan Moore, Michigan State University, 30 June 2017, the former British Prime Minister, Boris Johnson[who was born in America took class A drugs and conspired with a friend to beat up a journalist, during his time in office drastically clamped down on immigration, butallowed skilled migrants with a clean record to enter the country. He does not want criminals like himself to migrate to England. Manila Bulletin, The Nation's Leading Newspaper, published on 8 December 2019 by Reuters, reads:

Boris Johnson promised lower immigration if he wins power in an election..., but said he was not hostile to allowing foreigners to work and live in Britain overall

Johnson has promised a points-based approach to controlling immigration. He said his focus would be cutting down on unskilled migration, but that there would be scope for high skilled and other workers to come to Britain. The Prime Minster says:

"I'm not hostile to immigration ...I'm a believer in allowing people to come to this country and I think if they have talents and they want to do things and make their lives in the UK and they can contribute to our country – fantastic."

Therefore, 2020witnessed a restriction in migration while highly skilled people will be allowed to enter the country; as for criminals, they are being sent back to their homeland. And thus, Africans will continue contributing to the enrichment of the British economy through working, paying taxes, investing in businesses and in education, while their own countries remain impoverished.

Continuing with the subject of migration, African leaders, how long will you allow Europeans to continue to have discourse on how to solve African immigration to the West, a crisis that stems from the interference of a white presence in Africa, from the 1400s until the present? As I have previously mentioned, in order to protect their countries, millionaires such as Bill Gates have taken it upon themselves to speak out about how to reduce Africa's population in order to prevent African migration to Europe. This is according to an online article by Kichuu Info titled: *We Must Depopulate Africa To Save Europe*. These are the words of Mr Gates. In an interview with a German newspaper, Welt am Sonntag, Gates suggested that European nations must work together to reduce the population growth in Africa by committing more in overseas aid. The question is, what aid did he have in mind?

Going back to Mr Gates and his advice to depopulate Africa: what a statement to be uttered from the mouth of a man who is supposed be a humanitarian! Such a statement goes against humanity and human rights. An American by birth, Gates' interest is in Europe, not Africa, as his ancestry includes English, German, Irish and Scottish. I think he has forgotten that, if Africans had not migrated out of Africa over 3,000 years ago, there would perhaps not be any life in the western hemisphere today.

Jay Greenberg, who wrote the article in question, reminds us that, after Gates had called for European heads of state to give Africa aid to help depopulate its countries, 'Gates Foundation was accused of secretly sterilising millions of women in Africa via doctors in Kenya after abortion drugs were discovered in Tetanus vaccines'. He should have been arrested and put in prison perpetually. If a black man was accused of such a crime in America or England there is no question that he would be in prison. Greenberg asks the question: 'Could this have been a test for his proposed depopulation program?'

African leaders, how could you have allowed a psychopath with his crew to sterilise African women? Are you not aware of the history of the black woman? Even European leaders know that the mother of humanity is the African woman. Edward Wilmot Blyden (1832 to 1912), in his essays, gave African women the credit for being responsible for producing strong men who laboured for hundreds of years to create the wealth of Europe. Blyden would have been shocked to discover that, in 2020, African women and men are still labouring to maintain the economy and wealth of the western world. Africa's servitude to the west must cease!

According to David Owen, from the University of Warwick, England, the major factor underlying African migration to the UK is those who are seeking asylum. He goes on to assert that:

'The total number of asylum applications from Africa steadily increased throughout the 1990s, peaked in 2002, afterwards declining. The peak was 30.5 thousand in 2002. There were still 8.8 thousand applications in 2007.' Owen establishes the root of the cause by confirming that 'the bulk of asylum applications are from countries formerly colonised by the UK'. The largest source of asylum applications was from eastern and southern Africa, while the largest individual source was Somalia (43 thousand), followed by Zimbabwe (21 thousand), Congo and DR Congo (both 11.5 thousand), Nigeria (9.8 thousand) and Algeria(8.3 thousand).

https://*warwick.ac.*uk/*fac/soc/crer/events/*african/*confp_david_owen*

The unfortunate truth is that Africans are migrating to countries that have established racist institutions, which operate a systemic programme that is insidiously and invisibly racist in order to suppress the majority of black people in the West whilst allowing a minority to climb the social ladder to become leaders in order to benefit the west. In the western countries to which blacks are more likely to migrate, statistics show that such blacks are more likely to be committed to mental hospitals, while whites are offered alternative treatments, such as therapy or anti-depression tablets that are not addictive.

Statistics also show that blacks are more likely than their white counterparts to be imprisoned for minor crimes, while whites are given a warning or a community sentence. According to Black Law Enforcement of America, "black men make up the majority of those wrongfully convicted — approximately 49%. And since 1989, taxpayers have wasted $944 million to incarcerate black men and women that were later found to be innocent."

In British schools, black children are more likely to be excluded, especially boys, who are also more likely to be imprisoned as adults. Therefore, as it is in the mental hospitals, so it is in the prisons (although blacks are a minority in the western countries where they choose to live) When entering a prison, one may see more blacks than whites or the first person you see is either a black prisoner or a black member of staff.

In addition to the above, blacks are also more likely to be unemployed in the western countries where they despite being highly qualified and having a very good command of the English language. That said, their qualifications will never be good enough and so they are often forced to do further education to find work. They spend thousands on higher education, often just to stay in the country. Owen continues to inform us that 2.5 thousand students from Africa (1331 males, 1179 females) were accepted onto UK higher education courses in 2007/8.

My intention is not just to bring your attention to all the negative social elements of living in western countries. In highlighting the above, there are also many successful blacks living in the countries of their former colonisers who have managed to secure high-profile jobs and have a wealthy lifestyle, but they are a minority.

Let us work towards improving the socio-economic problems in Africa because no matter the negative reality of living in the western world, Africans who would have experienced extreme poverty in Africa have a better chance to improve their lives in the West. Often, some refuse to go back home or invest back home and would rather live and die in a foreign land, while others believe it is a duty to Mother Africa to remember her.

We would like Mother Africa to be a place from which her children migrate to other countries, not because of poverty, but because they want to travel and experience other cultures. Let Africa be a place where the natives want to stay, not run away from. Let Africa be a place for the natives to look to for prosperity and peace wherever they may go, whether it be north, west, south or east Africa.

Demand higher prices when trading; after all, it is Africa that supplies the world with its natural minerals. In order for Africa to successfully accomplish the above, put a stop to the mining of Africa's gold and diamonds to enrich the economies of the western world. Do not allow yourselves to be manipulated by the IMF and World Bank. Review the debt Africa owes the West. In my opinion, and I am sure many black activists and scholars would agree, Africa OWES NOTHING.

I will reiterate again the importance of encouraging Africans who live abroad to continue to invest in their homeland. Many would rather bank in western banks than African banks, as they have complained that funds go missing. We advise you to consider Ghana for the establishment of an international bank for Africans on the African continent and abroad. We suggest Ghana because, according to the Daily Mail, Ghana is ranked the most peaceful country in West Africa.

Africa cannot get world respect when some countries on the continent still pay colonial tax, even though we are liberated and free countries; it is a total disgrace and a shame. A United States of Africa can create a powerful military and political voice to put a stop to colonial tax and debts which are bribes. Instead, declare to the former colonisers (who still control some African countries' major utilities – water, electricity, telephone, transport, ports and major banks) that 2020 must see the end of exploitation of Africa at every level.

African leaders: demand compensation for the destruction of African civilisations during the times of the slave trade and colonial rule. I would like to remind you that after the Second World War, white Jews received compensation for four years of brutal murder when men, women, children and babies were forced into the gas chambers. Though I have sincere sympathy and empathy for the white Jews, Africans have received no compensation for nearly 400 years of kidnapping, slavery, rape, murder, and inhuman punishments, such as nailing an enslaved, pregnant female to the ground and beating her to death.

Moreover, let us not forget that Hitler also murdered Africans during the Second World War. According to Free Thought Project,

Hitler killed 10 million Africans, but no one knows exactly the number because Europeans erase it from history.

I ask you African leaders, how long will you allow Europeans to continue to exploit Africa, which is causing poverty, premature death and war throughout the continent? Africa must take control of its own land and resources and ensure that either the debt (which Africa does not owe) is written off or compensation is paid for slavery and the destruction of Africa. Encourage and instil African patriotism, nationalism, self-respect, racial pride and global respect. A United Africa is the future. Unite and start trading with each other more. African leaders, if you continue to lead with blind eyes, the women will unite and lead with open eyes.

Yours sincerely

Maisie Barrett

"The ends you serve that are selfish will take you no further than yourself but the ends you serve that are for all, in common, will take you into eternity."

Marcus Garvey

Bibliography

Diouf, Sylviane A: Fighting the Slave Trade: West African Strategies, Ohio University Press, United Kingdom (2003 and 2004)

Lynch, Hollis R, Blyden, Edward Wilmot: Pan-Negro Patriot, 1832-1912, Galaxy Books, published by Oxford University Press, New York (1912)

Robert, Lacey and Danziger, Danny: The Year 1000: What Life Was Like at the Turn of the First Millennium, Little Brown Book Group, Great Britain (1999)

Lynch, H. R. (ED) (1971): Black Spokesman, Selected Published Writings of Edward Wilmot Blyden, Frank Cass & Co

Wright, Bobby E: The Psychopathic Racial Personality and Other Essays, Third World Press, Chicago (1997)

COVID-19: Invest more in science, less in religion, Mrs Akeredolu tells Nigerians - TheNigeriaLawyer

https://www.legit.ng/1279025-buhari-western-culture-destroying-african-values-respect-elderly.html?utm_source=facebook&utm_medium=ps&fbclid=IwAR25CSU4sfYW7AHsIh2yD6IOxKLceoKzMg3TvWssjdnbbiNj44eJFxkuKLg

https://borgenproject.org/facts-about-poverty-in-the-democratic-republic-of-the-congo/

https://twitter.com/africaupdates

https://libertywritersafrica.com/how-european-and-american-governments-steal-from-africa-and-destabilize-african-economies/?fbclid=IwAR03iCR862RJrqgvvI7PimndKg5nEhuVdeDRFV6RalTETv5pwq86VVlbyo

https://www.dailymailgh.com/ghana-ranked-most-peaceful-country-in-west-africa/?fbclid=IwAR0-SHY3NUZ3PcBAyqm-POWloz21GOHsg6Uj68rIbxRqM4Gn63yq5ArAzOT8

https://thefreethoughtproject.com/hitler-killed-10-million-congo-erased/

https://qz.com/africa/1017926/china-has-overtaken-the-us-and-uk-as-the-top-destination-for-anglophone-african-students/

https://www.pambazuka.org/governance/france-still-robbing-its-former-african-colonies

https://answersafrica.com/countries-subjected-pay-colonial-tax-benefits-salvery-france.html

https://jubileedebt.org.uk/wp/wp-content/uploads/2018/09/Briefing_09.18.pdf

https://www.theguardian.com/world/2012/jan/22/poor-countries-debt-uk-interest

https://kichuu.com/bill-gates-depopulate-africa-save-europe/?fbclid=IwAR3b1ZaC8oM-Rxzk8kvTAxH6e9_qtUCd1if5lh1_rZkFaaU0lFPuwScEs_h4

https://www.cnbc.com/2018/06/27/china-increases-defence-ties-with-africa.html

END NOTES

[i] Message to the Founding Fathers of the OAU at their First Conference at Addis Ababa 1st May 1963 - Alhaji A E Cham-Joof". *The Point Newspaper*, 29 June 2006. Archived 23 November 2011 at the Wayback Machine
[ii] https://thecommonwealth.org/brexit-and-commonwealth

Printed in Great Britain
by Amazon